MACRAMÉ

A Beginner's Guide to Beautiful Handmade Projects for Home and Gardens. Includes Micro Macramé for Unique and Stylish Jewelry and Accessories.

by

Clara Cannon

Table of Contents

Introduction

Macramé is a form of textile, clothing that involves not the typical method of weaving or knitting but using a chain of knots. It is believed that it started in the thirteenth century in the western hemisphere with Arab weavers. They tied excess strings and yarn at the ends of hand-woven fabrics for towels, scarves, and shawls on decorative ends. Those Arab weavers used to travel in the desert to trade their handicrafts with city dwellers.

Over time, the huge craftsmanship spread across Europe and attracted the infatuation of everyone in the social classes. Indeed, "The masculine sailors of Macramé" are known to have engaged in craft while spending long months at sea. When they were at the port, the sailors sold their final ships so that they could purchase essential supplies before returning to their ships. Thus, the art of macramé continued to flourish.

Macramé's popularity peaked during the Victorian era. Macramé lace was all the rage and can be found on curtains, women's sleeves, dress edges, pillowcases, and anywhere else you can use the little lace.

Over the centuries, Macramé's popularity gradually declined. Soon some of the more detailed knot techniques were forgotten, leaving no record of their patterns and designs. However, the art of knitting a knot continues in life, and the passion for knots burns constantly beneath the surface.

Passion honored in the 1970s. During this decade, the macramé chunks were always seen everywhere. There was never a house without a macramé perch or a macramé owl hanging on its walls. During this period of revival, handicrafts focused more on textiles and furniture, such as hammocks, chairs, and decorative accessories made from his macramé used in the home. When the 1980s rocked and rolled, the macramé disappeared from people's memories.

However, this disappearance did not last long. With the 1990s, the grunge scene arose, and again the ancient ship witnessed a kind of rebirth, albeit this time in the form of hemp jewelry. Macramé bracelets and necklaces can be found in galleries and craft stores. The natural earthen hemp shape is the perfect complement to the complex art form.

Determining a period to learn macramé will depend on many factors, such as how quickly the technology is acquired. If you have been weaving or sewing for a long time, the degree of complexity should be much lower, as there are some similarities with the method.

Now, this ancient art form is resurrected again, but with a larger audience in mind. The world of haute couture started his experiment. In 2018, he was subtly added to the famous household clothing lines. This year you have seen macramé accessories in the spring and summer 2020 collections. Who would have thought that many beautiful macramé dresses would look like in the 2020 Spring Collection by Diane von Furstenberg, a well-known fashion designer?

Haute Couture's world has often led cavalry to revive crafts and techniques in the past year. The macramé potential cannot be denied as a complex art form in fashion. Macramé artists are slowly being recognized as professional craftsmen. So, take out your lace garter and start to hold!

Chapter 1. Types of Macramé Knots

Capuchin Knot

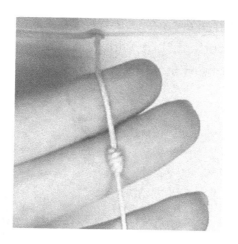

This knot for any project, and can be used as the foundation for the base of the project. Use lightweight cord for this – it can be purchased at craft stores or online, wherever you get your macramé supplies.

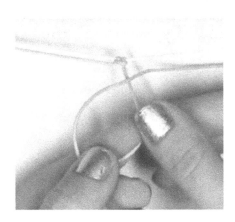

Watch the photos very carefully as you move along with this project, and take your time to make sure you are using the right string in the right point of the project.

Don't rush, and make sure you have even tension throughout. Practice makes perfect, but with the illustrations to help you, you'll find it's not hard at all to create.

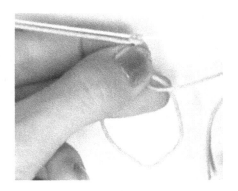

Start with the base cord, tying the knot onto this, and working your way along with the project.

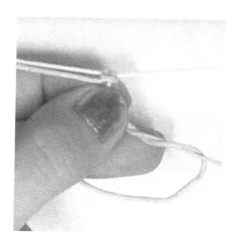

Twist the cord around itself 2 times, pulling the string through the center to form the knot.

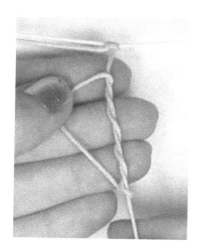

For the finished project, make sure that you have all your knots secure and firm throughout, and do your best to make sure it is all even. It is going to take practice before you are able to get it

perfectly each time, and with time, you are going to get it without too much trouble.

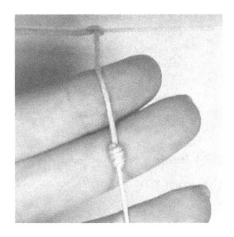

Make sure all is even and secure, and tie off. Snip off all the loose ends, and you are ready to go!

Crown Knot

This is a great beginning knot for any project, and can be used as the foundation for the base of the project. Use lightweight cord for this – it can be purchased at craft stores or online, wherever you get your macramé supplies.

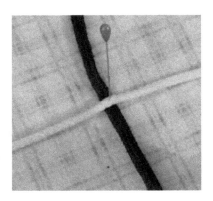

Watch the photos very carefully as you move along with this project, and take your time to make sure you are using the right string at the right point of the project.

Don't rush, and make sure you have even tension throughout. Practice makes perfect, but with the illustrations to help you, you'll find it's not hard at all to create.

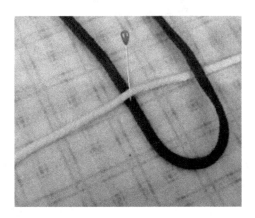

Use a pin to help keep everything in place as you are working.

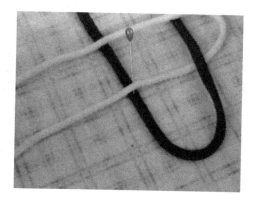

Weave the strings in and out of each other as you can see in the photos. It helps to practice with different colors to help you see what is going on.

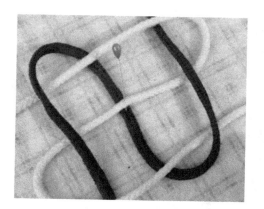 

Pull the knot tight, and then repeat for the next row on the outside.

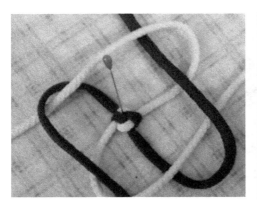 

Continue to do this as often as you like to create the knot. You can make it as thick as you like, depending on the project. You can also create more than one length on the same cord.

For the finished project, make sure that you have all your knots secure and firm throughout, and do your best to make sure it is all even. It is going to take practice before you are able to get it

perfectly each time, but remember that practice does make perfect, and with time, you are going to get it without too much trouble.

Make sure all is even and secure, and tie off. Snip off all the loose ends, and you are ready to go!

Diagonal Double Half Knot

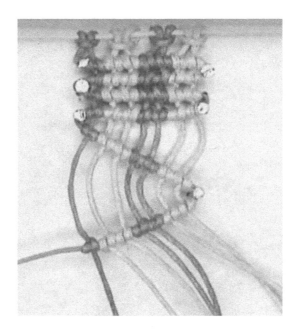

This is the perfect knot to use for basket hangings, decorations, or any projects that are going to require you to put weight on the project. Use a heavier weight cord for this, which you can find at craft stores or online.

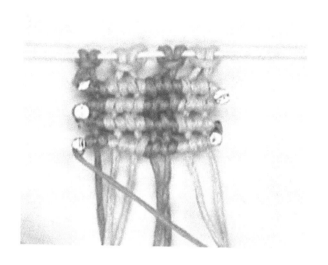

Watch the photos very carefully as you move along with this project, and take your time to make sure you are using the right string at the right point of the project.

Don't rush, and make sure you have even tension throughout. Practice makes perfect, but with the illustrations to help you, you'll find it's not hard at all to create.

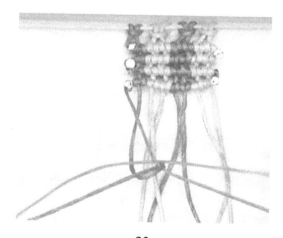

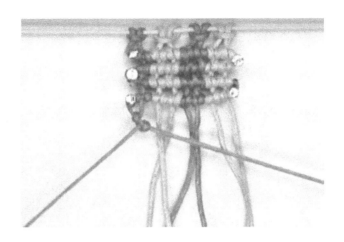

Start at the top of the project and work your way toward the bottom. Keep it even as you work your way throughout the piece. Tie the knots at 4-inch intervals, working your way down the entire thing.

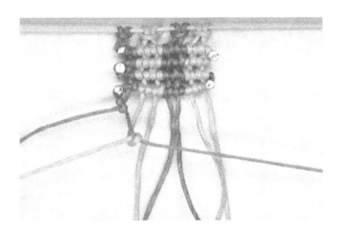

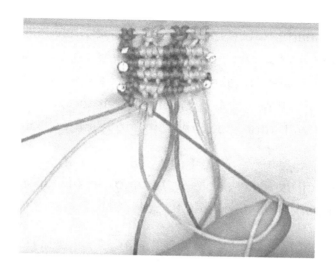

Weave in and out throughout, watching the photo as you can see for the right placement of the knots. Again, it helps to practice with different colors so you can see what you need to do throughout the piece.

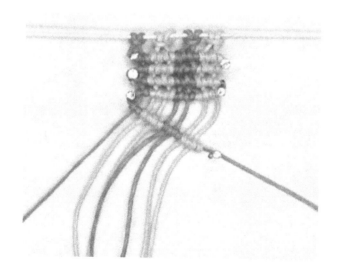

For the finished project, make sure that you have all your knots secure and firm throughout, and do your best to make sure it is all even. It is going to take practice before you are able to get it perfectly each time, but remember that practice does make perfect, and with time, you are going to get it without too much trouble.

Make sure all is even and secure, and tie off. Snip off all the loose ends, and you are ready to go!

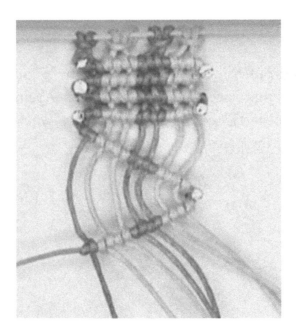

Frivolité Knot

This is a great beginning knot for any project, and can be used as the foundation for the base of the project. Use lightweight cord for this – it can be purchased at craft stores or online, wherever you get your macramé supplies.

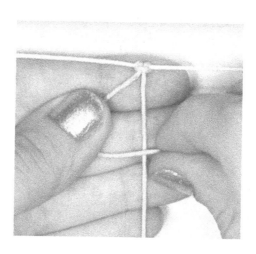

Watch the photos very carefully as you move along with this project, and take your time to make sure you are using the right string at the right point of the project.

Don't rush, and make sure you have even tension throughout. Practice makes perfect, but with the illustrations to help you, you'll find it's not hard at all to create.

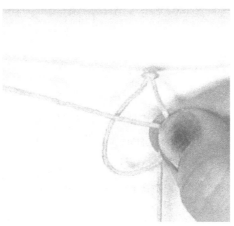

Use the base string as the guide to hold it in place, and then tie the knot onto this. This is a very straightforward knot, watch the

photo and follow the directions you see.

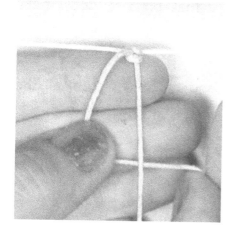 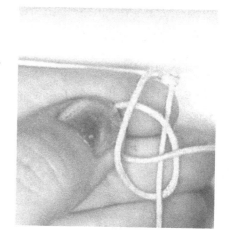

Pull the end of the cord up and through the center.

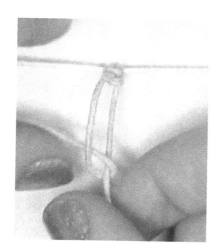 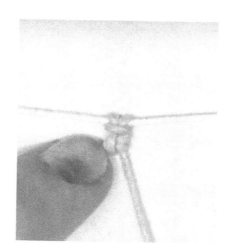

For the finished project, make sure that you have all your knots secure and firm throughout, and do your best to make sure it is all even. It is going to take practice before you are able to get it perfectly each time, but remember that practice does make perfect, and with time, you are going to get it without too much trouble.

Make sure all is even and secure, and tie off. Snip off all the loose ends, and you are ready to go!

Horizontal Double Half Knot

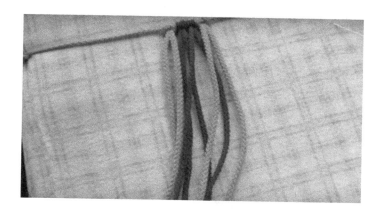

This is a great beginning knot for any project, and can be used as the foundation for the base of the project. Use lightweight cord for this – it can be purchased at craft stores or online, wherever you get your macramé supplies.

Watch the photos very carefully as you move along with this project, and take your time to make sure you are using the right string ta the right point of the project.

Don't rush, and make sure you have even tension throughout. Practice makes perfect, but with the illustrations to help you, you'll find it's not hard at all to create.

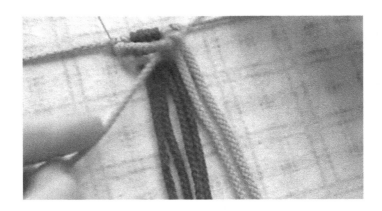

Start at the top of the project and work your way toward the bottom. Keep it even as you work your way throughout the piece. Tie the knots at 4-inch intervals, working your way down the entire thing.

For the finished project, make sure that you have all your knots secure and firm throughout, and do your best to make sure it is all even. It is going to take practice before you are able to get it

perfectly each time, but remember that practice does make perfect, and with time, you are going to get it without too much trouble.

Make sure all is even and secure, and tie off. Snip off all the loose ends, and you are ready to go!

Josephine Knot

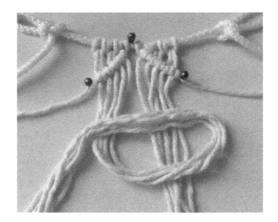

This is the perfect knot to use for basket hangings, decorations, or any projects that are going to require you to put weight on the project. Use a heavier weight cord for this, which you can find at craft stores or online.

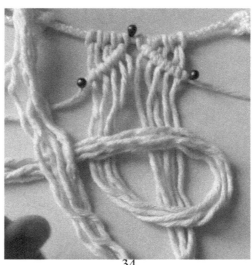

Watch the photos very carefully as you move along with this project, and take your time to make sure you are using the right string at the right point of the project.

Don't rush, and make sure you have even tension throughout. Practice makes perfect, but with the illustrations to help you, you'll find it's not hard at all to create.

Use the pins along with the knots that you are tying, and work with larger areas all at the same time. This is going to help you keep the project in place as you continue to work throughout the piece.

Pull the ends of the knots through the loops, and form the ring in the center of the strings.

For the finished project, make sure that you have all your knots secure and firm throughout, and do your best to make sure it is all even. It is going to take practice before you are able to get it perfectly each time, but remember that practice does make perfect, and with time, you are going to get it without too much trouble.

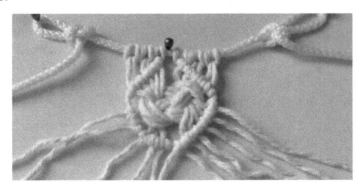

Make sure all is even and secure, and tie off. Snip off all the loose ends, and you are ready to go!

Lark's Head Knot

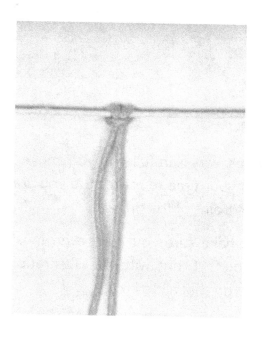

This is a great beginning knot for any project, and can be used as the foundation for the base of the project. Use lightweight cord for this – it can be purchased at craft stores or online, wherever you get your macramé supplies.

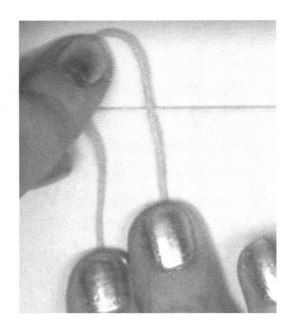

Watch the photos very carefully as you move along with this project, and take your time to make sure you are using the right string at the right point of the project.

Don't rush, and make sure you have even tension throughout. Practice makes perfect, but with the illustrations to help you, you'll find it's not hard at all to create.

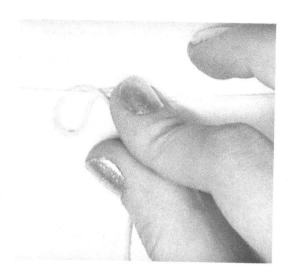

Use the base string as the core part of the knot, working around the end of the string with the cord. Make sure all is even as you loop the string around the base of the cord.

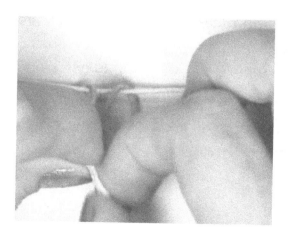

Create a slip knot around the base of the string and keep both ends even as you pull the cord through the center of the piece.

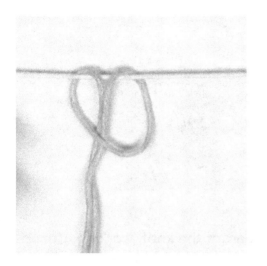 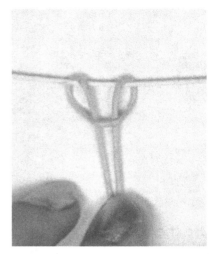

For the finished project, make sure that you have all your knots secure and firm throughout, and do your best to make sure it is all even. It is going to take practice before you are able to get it perfectly each time, but remember that practice does make perfect, and with time, you are going to get it without too much trouble.

Make sure all is even and secure, and tie off. Snip off all the loose ends, and you are ready to go!

PART I

Chapter 2. Suspended Projects

Now, it is time to learn how to make various home decors—simply by using the art of Macramé! Check them out and see which ones you want to make yourself!

Modern Macramé Hanging Planter

Plant hangers are really beautiful because they give your house or garden the feel of an airy, natural space. This one is perfect for condominiums or small apartments—and for those with minimalist, modern themes!

What you need:

- Plant
- Pot
- Scissors
- 50 ft. Paracord (Parachute Cord)
- 16 to 20 mm wooden beads

Instructions:

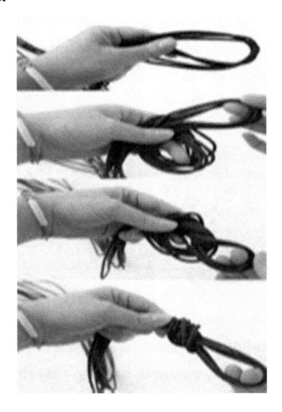

First, fold in half 4 strands of the cord and then loop so you could form a knot.

Now, divide the cords into groups of two and make sure to string 2 cords through one of the wooden beads you have on hand. String some more beads—at least 4 on each set of 2 grouped cords.

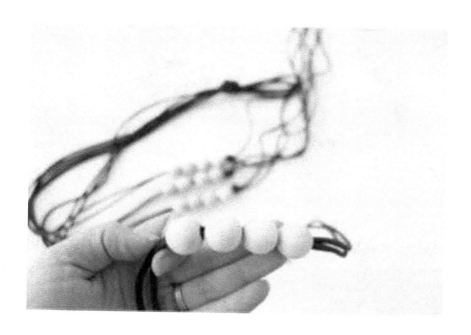

Then, measure every 27.5 inches and tie a knot at that point and repeat this process for every set of cords.

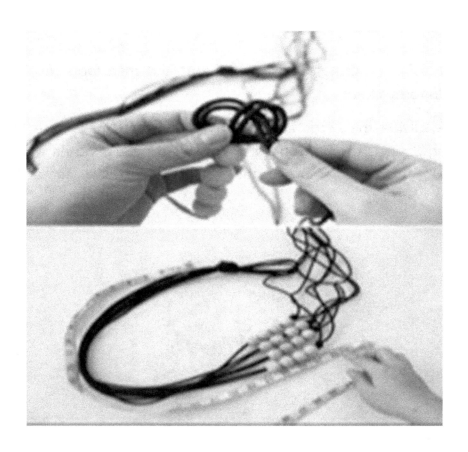

Look at the left set of the cord and tie it to the right string. Repeat on the four sets so that you could make at least 3″ from the knot you have made.

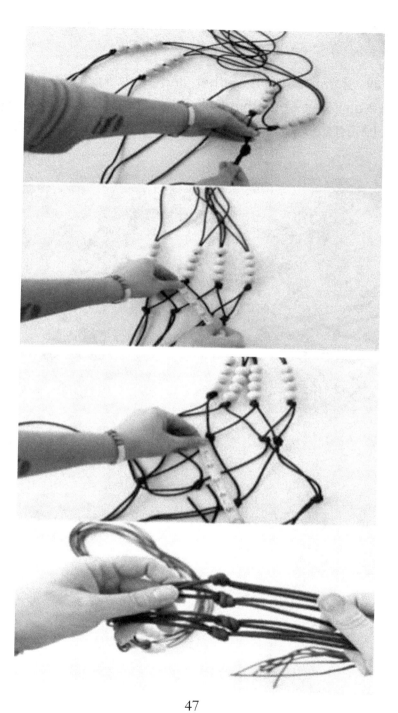

Tie another four knots from the knot that you have made. Make them at least 4.5″ each.

Group all of the cords together and tie a knot to finish the planter. You'll get something like the one shown below—and you could just add your very own planter to it!

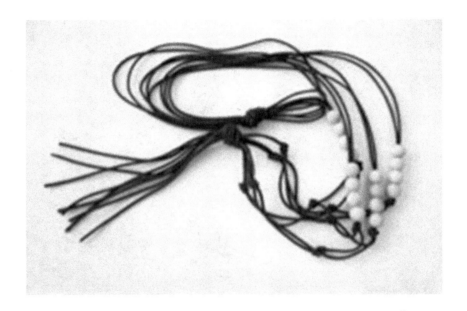

Mini Macramé Planters

Succulents are all the rage these days because they are just so cute and are really decorative! What's more is that you can make a lot of them and place them around the house—that will definitely give your place a unique look!

What you need:

- Small container
- Garden soil/potting mix
- Succulents/miniature plants
- ¼ inch jump ring
- 8 yards' embroidery thread or thin cord

Instructions:

Cut 36-inch of 8 lengths of cord. Make sure that 18 inches are already enough to cover enough half-hitches. If not, you can always add more. Let the thread loop over the ring and then tie a wrap knot that could hold all the cords together.

Create a half-twist knot by tying half of a square knot and repeating it multiple times with the rest of the cord.

Drop a quarter inch of the cord down and repeat step twice.

Arrange your planter and place it on the hanger that you have made.

Nail to the wall and enjoy seeing your mini-planter!

Amazing Macramé Curtain

Macramé Curtains give your house the feel of that beach house look. You don't even have to add any trinkets or shells—but you can, if you want to. Anyway, here's a great Macramé Curtain that you can make!

What you need:

- Laundry rope (or any kind of rope/cord you want)
- Curtain rod
- Scissors
- Pins
- Lighter
- Tape

Instructions:

Tie four strands together and secure the top knots with pins so they could hold the structure down.

Take the strand on the outer right part and let it cross over to the left side employing passing it through the middle. Tightly pull the strings together and reverse.

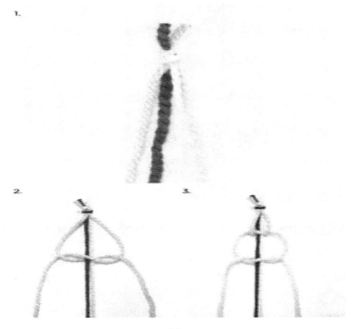

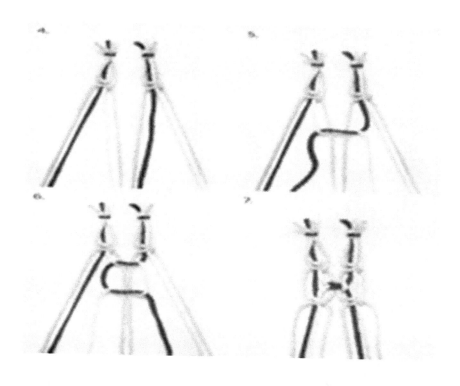

Repeat crossing the thread over four more times for the thread you now have in front of you. Take the strand on the outer left and let it pass through the middle, and then take the right and let it cross over the left side. Repeat as needed, and then divide the group of strands to the left, and also to the right. Repeat until you reach the number of rows you want.

You can now apply this to the ropes. Gather the number of ropes you want—10 to 14 is okay, or whatever fits the rod, with good spacing. Start knotting at the top of the curtain until you reach your desired length. You can burn or tape the ends to prevent them from unraveling.

Braid the ropes together to give them that dreamy, beachside effect, just like what you see below.

That's it; you can now use your new curtain!

Macramé Wall Art

Adding a bit of Macramé to your walls is always fun because it livens up the space without making it cramped—or too overwhelming for your taste. It also looks beautiful without being too complicated to make. You can check it out below!

What you need:

- Large wooden beads
- Acrylic paint
- Painter's tape
- Scissors
- Paintbrush
- Wooden dowel
- 70 yards' rope

Instructions:

Attach the dowel to a wall. It's best to just use removable hooks so you won't have to drill anymore.

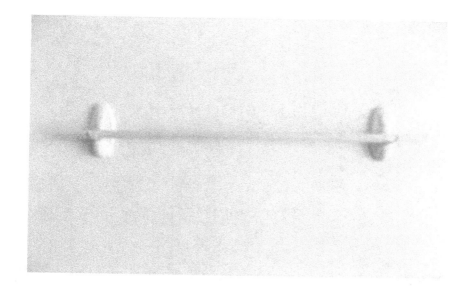

Cut the rope into 14 x 4 pieces, as well as 2 x 5 pieces. Use 5-yard pieces to bookend the dowel with. Continue doing this with the rest of the rope.

Then, start making double half-hitch knots and continue all the way through, like what's shown below.

Once you get to the end of the dowel, tie the knots diagonally so that they wouldn't fall down or unravel in any way. You can also add the wooden beads any way you want, so you'd get the kind of décor that you need. Make sure to tie the knots after doing so.

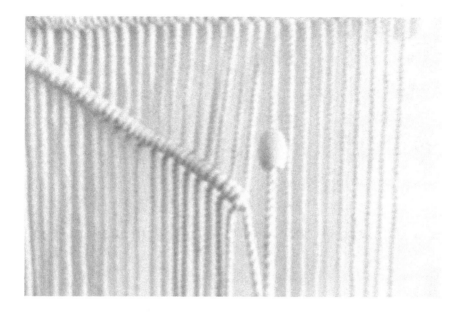

Use four ropes to make switch knots and keep the décor all the more secure. Tie around 8 of these.

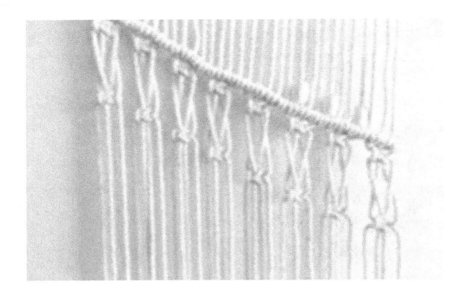

Add a double half hitch and then tie them diagonally once again.

Add more beads and then trim the ends of the rope.

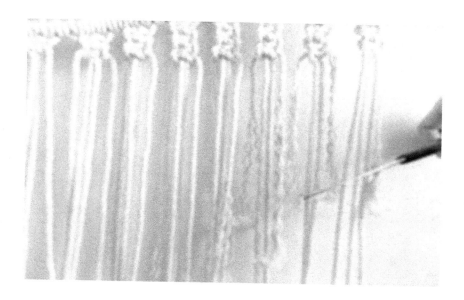

Once you have trimmed the rope, go ahead and add some paint to it. Summery or neon colors would be good.

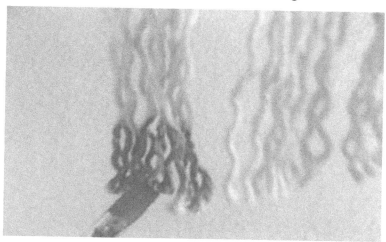

That's it! You now have your own Macramé Wall Art!

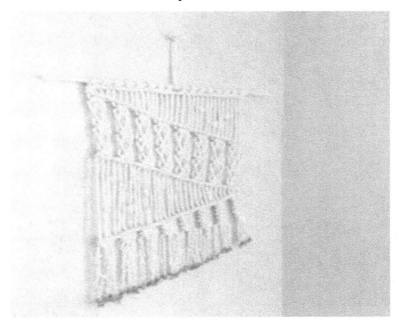

Hanging Macramé Vase

To add a dainty, elegant touch to your house, you could create a Macramé Vase. With this one, you'll have to make use of basket stitches/knots—which you'll learn about below. It's also perfect for those who really love flowers—and want to add a touch of nature at home!

What you need:

- Masking tape
- Tape measure or ruler
- 30 meters' thick nylon cord
- Small round vase (with around 20 cm diameter)

Instructions:

Cut eight cords measuring 3.5 yards or 3.2 meters each and set aside one of them. Cut a cord that measures 31.5 inches and set it aside, as well. Then, cut one cord that measures 55 inches.

Now, group eight lengths of cord together—the ones you didn't

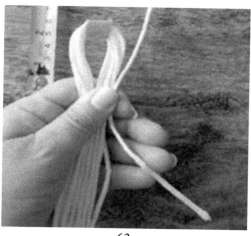

set aside, of course, and mark the center with a piece of tape.

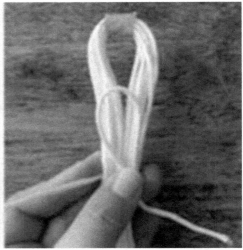

Wrap the cords by holding them down together and take around 80 cm of it to make a tail—just like what you see below.

Wrap the cord around the back of the long part and make sure to keep your thumb on the tail. Then, wrap the cord around the main cord group. Make sure it is firm, but don't make it too tight. If you can make the loop bigger, that would be good, too.

Do it 13 more times through the loop and go and pull the tail down so the loop could soften up. Stop letting the cords overlap by pulling them whenever necessary and then cut both ends so they would not be seen anymore.

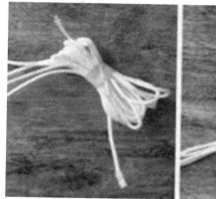

Divide the cords into groups of four and secure the ends with tape.

Get the group of cords that you have not used yet and make sure to measure 11.5 inches from the beginning—or on top. Do the overhand knot and get the cord on the left-hand side. Fold it over two of the cords and let it go under the cord on the right-hand side.

Fold the fourth cord and let it pass under the leftmost cord, then up the loop of the first cord. Make sure to push it under the large knot so that it would be really firm.

Make more half-hitches until you form more twists. Stop when you see that you have made around 12 of them and then repeat with the rest of the cords.

Now, it's time to make the basket for the vase. What you have to do here is measure 9 centimeters from your group of cords. Tie an overhand knot and make sure to mark with tape.

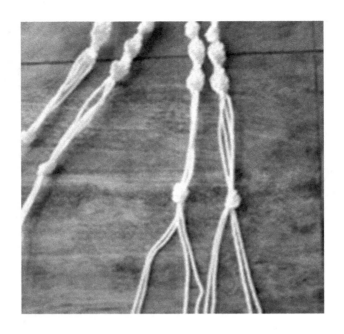

Let the two cord groups come together by laying them side by side.

Tie the cords down, but make sure to keep them flat. Make sure that the knots won't overlap, or else you'd have a messy project—which isn't what you'd want to happen. Use two cords from the left as a starting point and then bring the two cords on the right over the top of the loop. Loop them together under the bottom cords and then work them back up once more.

Now, find your original loop and thread the same cords behind them. Then, let them pass through the left-hand cords by making use of the loop once more.

Let the knot move once you already have it in position. It should be around 3 inches or 7.5 cm from the overhand knots. After doing so, make sure that you flatten the cords and let them sit to each other until you have a firm knot on top. Keep dividing and letting cords come together.

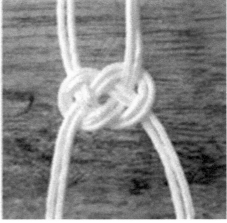

Get the cord on the left-hand side and let it go over the 2nd and 3rd cords before folding the fourth one under the first two cords. You'd then see a square knot forming between the 2nd and 3rd cords. You should then repeat the process on the right-hand side. Open the cord on the right side and let it go under the left-hand cord. Repeat this process thrice, and then join the four-square knots that you have made by laying them out on a table.

You'll then see that the cords have come together at the base. Now, you have to start wrapping the base by wrapping a 1.4-meter cord and wrap around 18 times.

To finish, just cut the cords the way you want. It's okay if they're not of the same length so that there'd be variety—and they'd look prettier on your wall. Make sure to tie overhand knots at the end of each of them before placing the vase inside.

Enjoy your new hanging vase!

Chapter 3. More Suspended Projects - 1

A Macramé Inside Decoration

A Macramé inside decoration is a simple DIY venture that will add a high-quality touch to any room in your home. This free instructional exercise will assist you with making a tapestry with a great deal of intriguing examples, for example, spirals and triangles. Try not to be reluctant to switch things up to make it your own.

In spite of what it looks like, this is a basic undertaking that will simply take you an hour or two to finish. It truly meets up quickly and you'll discover loads of chances to add your own style to it.

This is only one of many free Macramé designs that incorporate plant holders, bookmarks, shades, and a ton more.

The bunches you'll be utilizing for this Macramé inside decoration incorporate Lark's Head tie, Spiral bunch, and Square bunch. You can figure out how to tie every one of these bunches by perusing our guide on the best way to Macramé.

What You'll Need:

- Macramé line, scissors, and a wooden dowel on a table
- Cotton Macramé Cord (200 feet or 61 meters)
- Wooden Dowel (3/4-inch measurement, 24 inches in length)
- Scissors

I'm utilizing cotton clothesline for my Macramé line. It has a magnificent normal look to it and is genuinely reasonable.

The wooden dowel shouldn't be these careful measurements and instead of the wooden dowel, utilize whatever size you like as long as you can fit all the ropes over it. If you'd prefer to give it a progressively outdoorsy feel, you could utilize a tree limb about a similar size.

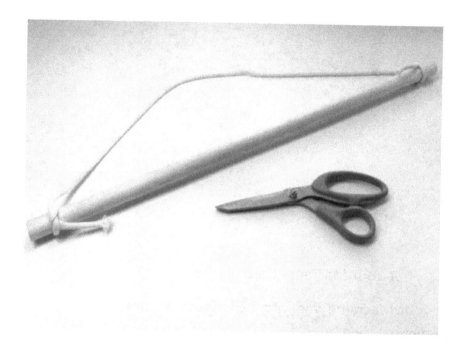

1. Make a Hanger for Your Wooden Dowel

Cut a bit of Macramé rope that is three feet (one meter). Tie each end of the string to the different sides of the wooden dowel.

You'll utilize this to hang your Macramé venture when it's done. I like to connect it to the start so I can hang the Macramé venture as I tie ties. Working along these lines is a lot simpler than laying it down.

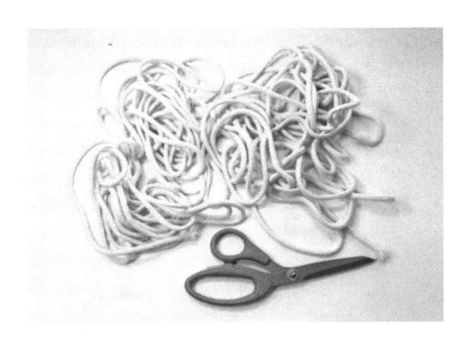

2. Cut Your Macramé Cord

Cut your Macramé line into 12 lengths of rope that are 15 feet (4.5 meters) long.

This may appear to be a great deal of line yet hitches take up more rope than you would might suspect. It is highly unlikely to make your rope longer if you have to, so it's smarter to cut more than you'll utilize.

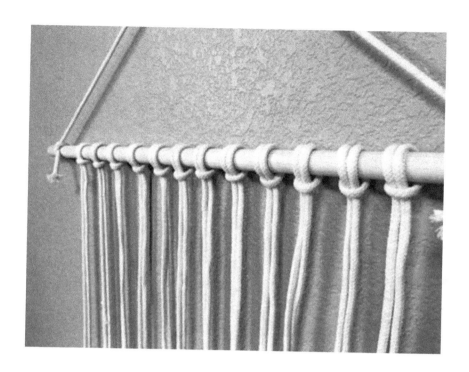

3. Append Macramé Cord to Dowel

Warbler's head hitch on a wooden dowel.

Crease one of the Macramé strings into equal parts and utilize a warbler's head bunch to append it to the wooden dowel.

Join the various strings similarly.

4. Bunch Spiral Stitches

A Macramé winding join.

Take the initial 4 ropes and make a left-confronting winding join (additionally called a half bunch sinnet) by tying 13 half bunches.

5. Keep Knotting Spiral Stitches

Six winding lines.

Utilize the following arrangement of four ropes to make another winding fasten with 13 half bunches. Keep working in bunches with four lines. At the point when you finish, you ought to have an aggregate of six winding fastens.

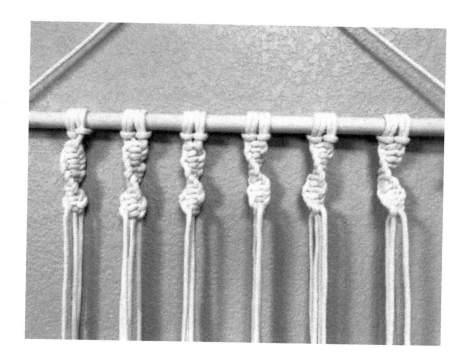

6. Make Square Knots

A lot of square bunches.

Measure roughly two creeps down from the last bunch in the winding fasten. This is the place you're going to put your next bunch, the square bunch.

Utilizing the initial four ropes, make a correct confronting square bunch. Keep making the correct confronting square bunches right over this line. Give a valiant effort to keep them all on a level plane even with one another. You'll wind up with a lot of six square bunches.

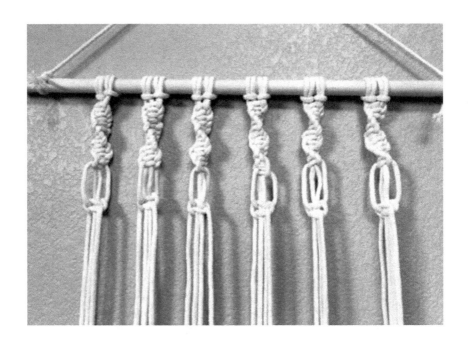

7. Lessening Square Knots

A second line of square bunches.

Presently it's a great opportunity to begin diminishing the square bunches so we can have a "V" state of bunches.

Leave the initial two lines and the last two lines free. Make right confronting square bunches with each gathering of four. You'll presently have a second column with the two first and two last lines unknotted and five square bunches.

It doesn't make a difference how you space these; simply keep them even with one another for each line.

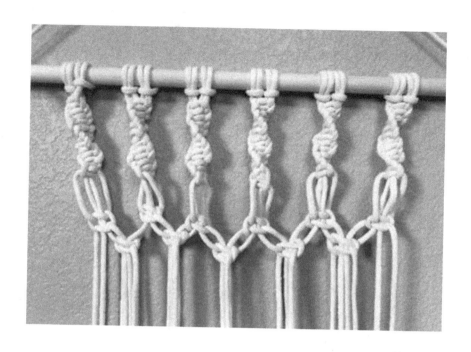

8. Keep Decreasing the Square Knots

A "V" made out of square bunches.

In the third line, you're going to forget about the initial four strings and the last four ropes. You'll have four square bunches.

For the fourth line forget about six strings toward the start and six ropes toward the end. You'll have three square bunches.

In the fifth line, you'll forget about eight lines toward the start and eight additional lines toward the end. You'll have two square bunches now.

For the 6th and last line, you'll forget about 10 strings toward the start and 10 ropes toward the end. This will leave you with four lines to make one last square bunch.

9. Increment Square Knots

Making a second "V' with square bunches.

Time for all the more square bunches! This time, we will be expanding them to shape a triangle, or a tops turvy "V."

For the primary line of this segment, forget about the initial eight and last eight strings. You'll make two square bunches.

In the third column, forget about six lines toward the start and the end. You'll have three square bunches right now.

For the fourth line, forget about four strings toward the start and four toward the end. You'll have four square bunches.

In the fifth line, forget about two strings toward the start and the last two ropes. Presently you'll have five square bunches right now.

For the last column, utilize all the lines to make ties. You'll have six square bunches for this column.

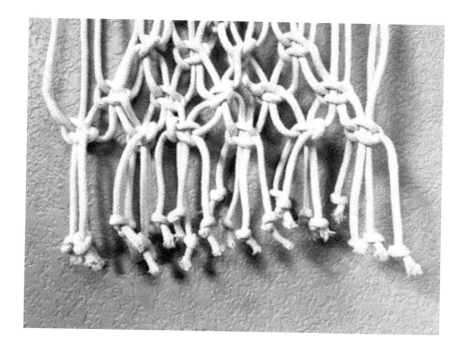

10. Trim and Knot

Overhand bunches.

Time to give your Macramé tapestry a decent trim. Leave some space (around six to eight inches) under your last line. Utilize your scissors to cut the lines straight over.

Chapter 4. More Suspended Projects - 2

Learn macramé with step by step instructions accompanied by real knot pictures.

Plant Hanger Ayla

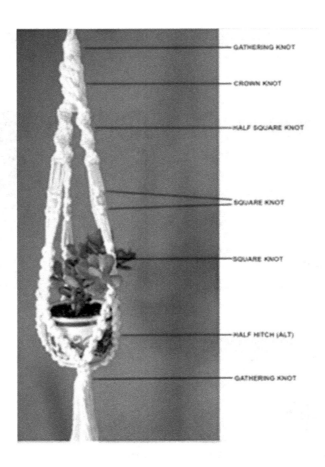

GATHERING KNOT

CROWN KNOT

HALF SQUARE KNOT

SQUARE KNOT

SQUARE KNOT

HALF HITCH (ALT)

GATHERING KNOT

Description: Plant hanger of 2 feet and 3, 5 inches (70 cm)

Used Knots: Square knot, half square knot, alternating square knot, crown knot, gathering knot, and half hitch knot.

Supplies: 4 strands of a cord of 13 feet and 1, 5 inches (4 meters), 4 strands of 16 feet and 4, 8 inches (5 meters), 2 strands of 3 feet and 3, 4 inches (1 meter), 1 wooden ring of 2 inches (50 mm) and 4 wooden beads: diameter 0, 4 inches (10mm)

Directions (step-by-step):

1. Fold the 8 longer strands of cord in half through the wooden ring. Tie all (now 16) strands together with 1 shorter strand of 3 feet and 3,4 inches (1 m) with a gathering knot. Cut the cord ends off after tying the gathering knot.

2. Now follows the crown knot. It is the easiest when you turn your project up-side-down in between your legs, as shown in the photos. Divide the 16 strands into 4 sets of 4 strands each. Each set has 2 long strands and 2 shorter strands. Tie 5 crown knots in each set. Pull each strand tight and smooth.

3. Tie 15 half square knots on each set of four strands. In each set, the 2 shorter strands are in the middle and you are tying with the 2 outer, longer strands. Dropdown 2, 4 inches (6 cm of no knots).

4. Tie 1 square knot with each set.

5. Then add the wooden bead to the 2 inner cords of each set and tie 1 square knot with each set again. Dropdown 2, 4 inches (6 cm of no knots) and tie 6 square knots with each of the 4 sets.

6. Take 2 strands of 1 set and make 10 alternating half hitch knots. Repeat for the 2 left strands of that set. And then repeat for all sets.

7. Tie an alternating square knot to connect the left two cords in each set with the right two of the set next to it, followed by 3 square knots for each new set (so you have 4 square knots in total for each new-formed set).

8. Place your chosen container/bowl into the hanger to make sure it will fit, gather all strands together and then tie a gathering knot with the left-over shorter strand of 3 feet and 3,4 inches (1 m). Trim all strands to the length that you want. If you want, you can unravel the ends of each strand.

Plant Hanger Bella

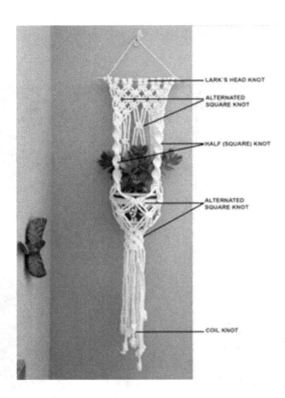

Description: Plant hanger of 60 cm (not counting the fringe)

Supplies: 6 strands of the cord of 13 feet and 1, 5 inches (4 meters), 4 strands of 16 feet and 4, 8 inches (5 meters) and a wooden stick of 11, 8 inches (30cm)

Used Knots: A half knot, Lark's Head knot, (Alternating) square knot and Coil knot

Directions (step-by-step):

1. Fold all strands in half and tie them to the wooden stick with a Lark´s Head knot. The long strands are on the outer side (2 strands on the left side and 2 on the right).

2. Make 4 rows of alternating square knots. (See knot guide for explanation)

3. In the 5th row, you only make 2 alternating square knots on the right and 2 on the left.

4. In the 6th row, you only tie 1 alternating square on each side.

5. Then, with the 4 strands on the side, you tie 25 half (square) knots. Do this for sides, the left and right sides.

6. Take 4 strands from the middle of the plant hanger, first drop down 2, 4 inches (6 cm of no knots), and then tie a square knot with the 4 center strands. Now with the 4 strands next to the middle, drop down 3, 15 inches (8 cm of no knots), and tie a square knot. Do this for both sides (left and right).

7. Dropdown 2, 4 inches (6 cm of no knots) and tie 2 (alternated) square knots by taking 2 strands from both sides (right and left group). Then 3 alternating square knots with the other groups. These knots must be about at the same height where the strands with the half knots have ended.

8. Take the 2 outer strands of the left group, which you made 25 half knots, and take the 2 outer strands of the group on the right. First dropping down 2, 4 inches (6 cm of no knots), you tie a square knot with these 4 strands.

9. Do the same with the rest of the strands leftover, make groups of 4 strands and tie alternated square knots on the same height as the one you made in step 8. Dropdown 2, 4 inches (6 cm of no knots), and make another row of alternated square knots using all strands.

10. Dropdown 2, 4 inches (6 cm of no knots) and make 5 rows of alternated square knots. Be careful: this time leaves NO space in between the alternated square knots and you make them as tight as possible.

11. Dropdown as many inches/cm as you want to make the fringe and tie at all ends a coiled knot.

12. Then cut off all strands, directly under each coil knot.

Plant Hanger Cathy

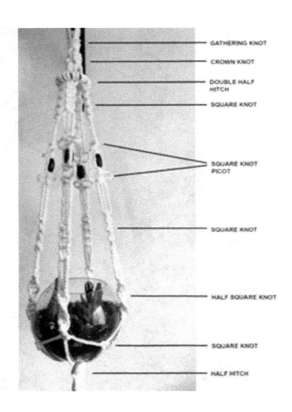

GATHERING KNOT
CROWN KNOT
DOUBLE HALF HITCH
SQUARE KNOT
SQUARE KNOT PICOT
SQUARE KNOT
HALF SQUARE KNOT
SQUARE KNOT
HALF HITCH

Description: Plant hanger of 2 feet and 9, 5 inches (85 cm) - not counting the fringe

Supplies: 4 wooden beads of 1,2 inches (3cm), 3 inches (7,5cm) wooden ring, 4 cords of 18 feet (5,5 meter), 2 cords of 15 feet (4,5 meter) and 1 cord of 2 feet and 1,6 inches (65 centimeters)

Used Knots: Gathering knot, crown knot, (double) half hitch, (Half) square knot and Square knot

Directions (step-by-step):

1. Fold the 6 longest cords in half, placing the loops neatly side by side. Use a gathering knot for tying the cords together with the shortest cord. This gives you twelve cords in total.

2. Arrange the cords in four groups of three cords each. Make sure that each group consists out of 2 longer cords and 1 shorter cord. Tie three Chinese Crown knots with the four groups of cords.

3. Slip the wooden ring over the top loop and drop it down 1, 2 inches (3 cm) from the last Chinese Crown knot. With each of the twelve cords, tie one double half hitch on the ring to secure it. This gives you a ring of double half hitches.

4. Arrange the cords into four groups of three cords each. The middle cord of each group is the shorter one; this is called the filler cord. Repeat step five thru eight for each group.

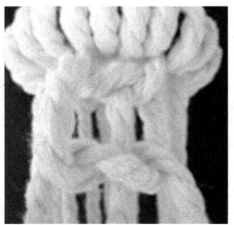 

5. Tie four square knots, each having one shorter, filler cord.

6. Skip down 2 inches (5 cm). Tie one square knot picot.

7. Slide a bead up the filler cord. Tie another square knot picot directly under the bead.

8. Skip down 2 inches (5 cm). Tie five square knots, each having one filler cord.

9. Skip down 2 inches (5 cm). Tie 10 half square knots, each having one filler cord.

10. Repeat the following procedure for each of the four groups you have just knotted: skip down 2, 4 inches (6 cm); take one cord from each neighboring square knot to tie a square knot WITHOUT a filler cord. This gives you four square knots made of two cords each. The cords in the middle of each group are NOT used to knot.

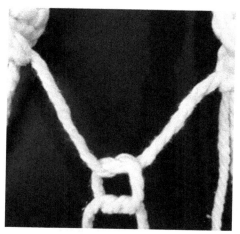

11. Skip down 4, 8 inches (12 cm). Gather and tie all cords together with one of cords hanging using to tie 10 times a half hitch. 12. Cut the fringe to measure 6 inches (15 cm).

Chapter 5. Another Suspended Project

Wreath of Nature

Just imagine having a Macramé wreath in your home! This one is inspired by nature and is one of the most creative things you could do with your time!

What you need:

- Clips or tape
- Fabric glue
- Wreath or ring frame
- 80 yards 12" cords
- 160 yards 17-18" cords
- 140 yards 14-16" cords
- 120 yards 12-13" cords

Instructions:

1.   Mount the cords on top of the wreath and make the crown knot by folding one of the cords in half. Let the cords pass through the ring and then fold a knot and make sure to place it in front of the ring. Let the loops go over the ring and pull them your way so they could pass the area that has been folded.

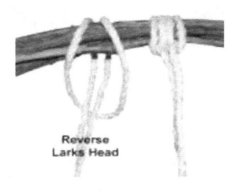

Reverse
Larks Head

2.   Let the ends pass over the first loop so you could make way for some half-hitches. Let them go over and under the ring, and then tightly pull it over the cord. This way, you'd get something like the one below. Repeat these first few steps until you have mounted all the cords on top of the ring. Organize them in groups of ten.

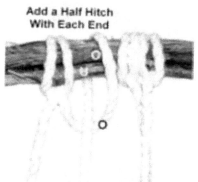

Add a Half Hitch
With Each End

3.   Now, you can make leaf-like patterns. To do this, make sure to number the first group of cords on the right side and make half-hitches in a counter-clockwise direction. Take note that you have to horizontally place the holding plate. If you see that it has curved slightly, make sure to reposition it and then attach cords labeled 5 to 7. Move it to resemble a diagonal position and then attach cords 8 to 10.

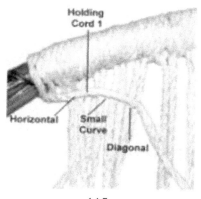

Holding
Cord 1

Horizontal   Small
Curve

Diagonal

115

4.   Make sure knots have been pushed close together and then use the cord on the leftmost corner to lower the leaf-like portion. The first four cords should be together on the handle and then go and attach cords labeled 3 to 6 to the holding cord. Move the cords so they'd be in a horizontal position.

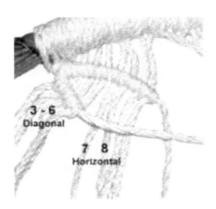

5.   Now, move the cord upwards so that the center would not curve unnecessarily. Repeat the process for the cords on the bottom part of the frame and then start making the branches by selecting 2 to 4 cords from each of the leaves. Don't select the first and second row's first and last leaves.

6.   Hold the cords with tape or clips as you move them towards the back of the design and decide how you want to separate—or keep the branches together. Secure the cords with glue after moving them to the back.

7.   Wrap the right cords around the ones on the left so that branches could be joined together. Make sure to use half-hitches to wrap this portion and then use a set of two cords to create a branch.

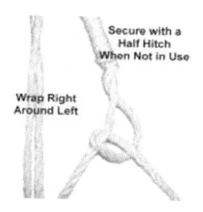

8.   Let the branches intertwine by checking the plan that you have written earlier and then use half-hitches again to connect the branches together. Together with your previous wrap, make use of another wrap and make sure they all come together as one.

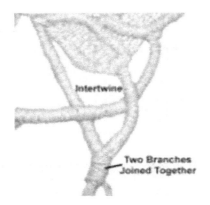

9.   Secure the bundle by wrapping a 3-inch wrap cord around it and then let it go over the completed knot.

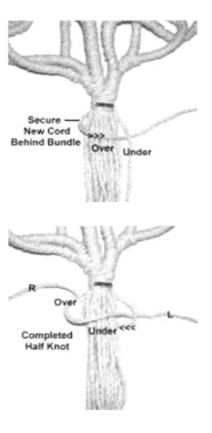

118

10.   As for the fringe, you have to divide the knots into groups of two and make sure to tie a half-hitch on the rightmost cord on the left, and then let them alternate back and forth continuously under you have managed to cover your whole wreath. Let each sinnet slide under the whole wreath and then attach each cord to the ring itself.

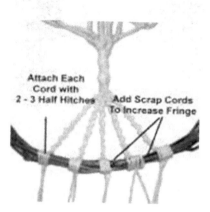

11.   Next, make sure to divide the cords into small groups and then use the cords so you could tie the overhand knots. Unravel the fibers so you could form a wavy fringe.

That's it! You now have your own Macramé Wreath of Nature!

Macramé Skirt Hanger

Well, it's not really a skirt hanger. But, it's something that could spruce up your closet or your walls. It gives the room that dainty, airy feeling. You could also use it for plant pots that are at least 8 inches in size.

What you need:

- 12 mm size beads
- One 8-inch ring
- One 2-inch ring
- 4mm cord

Instructions:

1.   First, cut 8 cords that are at least 8.5 yards long then cut a cord that's 36 inches long before cutting 4 more yards of cord.

2.   Then, fold the 8.5 yards in half to start the top section of the thread. Let it pass through the ring and let some parts drape down before choosing two cords from outside the bundle. Make sure to match the ends and then try the square knot.

3.   To bundle the locks, you should find the center and move 8 inches down from it and then stop when you reach 12 inches.

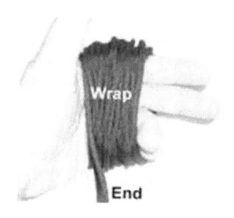

4. Wrap the center a couple of times and then pull the ends tightly until you build a sturdy bundle, and then tug on the ends so that the roll could get smaller.

Pass End
Under Last Coil
to Secure

5. Make a total of four spirals that could at least be 20 inches and then manage the filler cords by adding a bead to them.

6. To make the basket, attach the cords to the 8-inch ring by using double half-hitch stitches and then arrange the cords so they could be in four groups. Pull the stitches tightly so there's enough spacing and then mount all of the cords to the ring in a counter-clockwise motion. To cover the ring, make sure to tie a half-hitch at each end.

7. Then, make alternating square knots just below the ring and divide into two groups of 40 strings each—it sounds like a lot but it's what would naturally happen. Add some tape to the cords you have labeled 1 to 40 and then tie a half-square knot to the four injected threads. Add some beads, and then tie a knot again.

8.   Add beads to cords 20 to 21 after using cords 19 to 22 and then make alternating square knots and then repeat on the cords on the backside. Add beads and make more alternating square knots, then add beads to cords 16 to 17 after using cords labeled 15 to 18. Tie the next row without adding any beads and then use cords 11 to 30. Work on cords 12 to 29 by adding beads to them and making use of alternating square knots. Repeat the 3rd row with no beads and the 4th row with beads and choose four of your favorite cords to make fringes.

9.   Speaking of fringes, number the remaining cords mentally and then add a succession of 2 to 3 beads for each layer (i.e., 2/4/6 or 3/6/9) and then trim all the cords evenly.

Enjoy your new Skirt Hanger!

Macramé Speaker Hanger

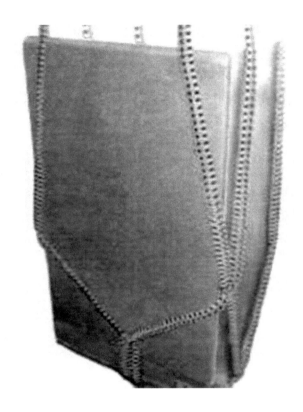

Finally, you could also make a Macramé Speaker Hanger! This is perfect for keeping those laptop or computer speakers in place!

What you need:

- Measuring tape
- Fabric glue
- Brass rings
- 50 yards Paracord

Instructions:

1.   Cut 16 cords that are 15 yards long, and then cut 2 cords that are 2 yards long, and finally, cut 2 cords that are 60 inches long.

2.   What you have to do is wrap the two rings together using 2 cords and by tying with the crown knot. Make use of half hitch stitches to secure the wrap and then find the center of the cord. Make sure to secure them on the surface and to hold them close together. 8 of the two cords should then be lined up in a central manner so that they'd be able to hold the speaker.

3.   Now, go and bundle the long cords by wrapping and pulling them tightly together and letting the first end pass under the last coil. Wrap securely so it would not unravel.

4.   Make sure to pull more cords from the bundles and then tighten the wraps on the center with your working cords. Let the lower portion come together by using square knots and make sure that you go and tighten the first half of it. Tie the second half around the board and then turn the board around after you have let the rolled coils pass through at one end of the ring.

5.   Use half-hitches to arrange the center and let the rolled bundles dangle at the other end of the ring. Fold the sennit so you could match it with the last couple of knots, and then wrap the scrap cord around it. Now, put the hanger horizontally on your workspace and secure with square knots.

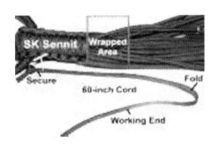

6.   Let the working end pass through the middle of the bundle and then bring the working end around the bundle that you are using. Let it pass over the front and under the cord's back and keep wrapping as firmly as you can until you see something that looks like a loop.

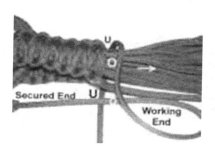

7.   Take the pin away from the secured end and pull until you reach the knot inside. Make use of fabric glue to coat this with and trim the ends. Let flame pass through it to secure it, as well.

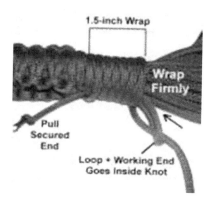

8.   Tie 5 half knots to keep the hanger secure and start suspending on the wall or ceiling—whichever you prefer. Place some beads before tying the knot again, and then make use of previous fillers as working cords before firmly tightening the knot. Create 25 more square knots and push the knots up to eliminate spooling. Repeat process until your desired length.

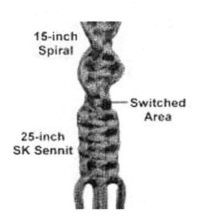

9.   Finally, make a figure-eight knot and make sure to pull the end tightly before tying several more. It depends on how much you want to see. Heat the fuse and apply glue to keep your project secure!

Enjoy your new speaker hanger!

PART II

Chapter 6. Horizontal Project

Pillow

Now we will learn how to create this beautiful DIY Macramé Pillow. It's not as complicated as it looks– the toughest part is to cut the long cords.

Knots used:

- Lark Head Knot
- Square Knot
- Double Half Hitch Knot

Materials Needed:

- Macramé Cord
- Sewing Machine/Thread (optional)
- Dowel or Stick
- Scissors
- Pillow cover and insert
- Tape Measure

You can start with your pillow cover you have for this pillow, or create a simple pillow cover for any pillow available. Don't just make it yet-see first Stage no 5. In the illustration below, the pillow cover is made of drop fabric. This ended up exactly identical to the rope, which looks impressive.

However, if you do want to see the Macramé show, pick a different color for your pillow cover.

The cover in the picture is 20 x 20 inches, for reference. You have to ensure that your Macramé pattern can cover your pillow-but if not. The best news is if required, it can be stretched out.

Step by Step Instructions:

1. 12-foot string.

2. Using reverse lark's head knots tie all 16 cords to the dowel. You've learned how to tie a lark head knot to build the hat in the previous instructions.

3. For this cover, the pattern is the only rows of alternating square knots. Leave a little gap among each knot-around half of an inch as a reference. Having a little space makes the project run even quicker.

You have to keep making the alternating square knots till you get down to the 20 " edge. Measure using the tape to watch where you are.

Create two horizontal rows of (left-to-right, then right-to-left) double half-hitch knots until you touch down the bottom.

4. So, now that we're done with the design cut off the excess from the bottom, but keep a piece of the fringe – about 5 inches or so. You may leave more or less; it's entirely up to you.

So, you are either going to remove your pattern from the rod or just cut it off.

5. Break it off. Here's how you stick the Macramé design to your pillow. Before you stitch it up, whether you're making a cover by yourself – you're necessarily going to line up the design to the facade of the cover, leaving the cut edges a little over the top hang.

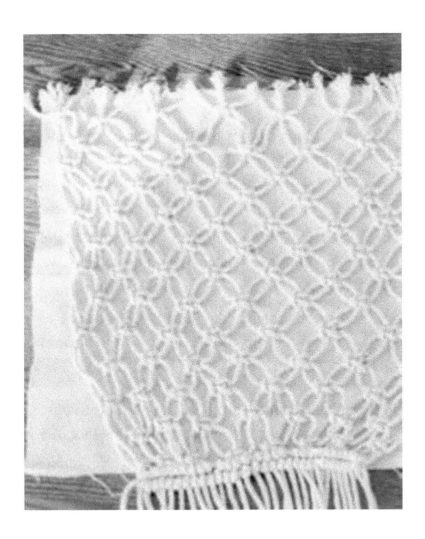

6. Place the back part over the cover, and Macramé design-right sides are facing each other-essentially you make a sandwich, and the Macramé design is called the "meat."

So, now patch your pillow cover's top edge-go above the cords too! Then it takes some degree of finesse, however you can fix it. Pin it all down to hold it all together.

Shove the Macramé pattern within your pillow to stitch the rest of your pillow cover and stitch the remaining seams as usual.

7. Take another length of the Macramé cord and tie an easy knot on the back to attach the rest of the cover. Loop this string from out and in of square knots. Not only does this help spread out your pattern. Yet it must protect it down to the bottom too.

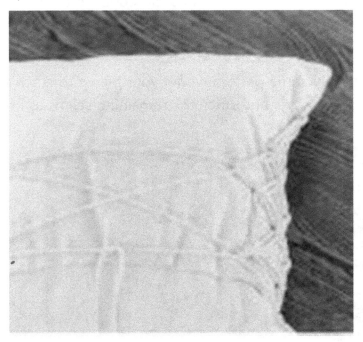

That is it! At the bottom edge of your pillow, the fringes will hang.

For A Ready Made Pillow Cover: You can open one of the joints and follow the instructions above or simply take the other piece of Macramé cord and thread it around the top. Then twist it backward. As mentioned above, you can also tie the sides.

Or, you could even hand stitch it to your pillow cover that certainly gives your sofa or easy chair a bit of an oomph. Yet this is sort of a novelty cushion – laying your head on it is kind of uncomfortable.

Chapter 7. More Horizontal Project

Window Belt

Window Belt has diamonds in the middle that are created with a traditional method. To create an oval-shaped opening in the middle of each of the diamonds, the strings are folded. The end is the braided knot.

This Macramé project is relatively moderate. You must need some practice for creating diamonds before you successfully creating this pattern.

Material Needed:

- 2mm String Material
- Project Board
- Tape
- Pins

Knots used:

- Doubled Half Hitch
- Overhand Knot
- Interlaced Plaits
- Vintage Diamonds

Preparation:

For making the Window Belt, the first step is measuring the hips or waists. Cut twelve working cords, about four times the span you've just measured. Fix the edges with gum or an Overhand knot for all the cords. Cut two holding strings, each of which is at least one and a half times the span you are creating. Prepare these cables with the tape so that they can be clearly identified. Set all the working strings vertical, in two sets of six cords. The holding cord should be put among the two sets.

Define the middle by horizontally placing a section of tape over the region. You must start in the middle for the first interval of the Belt, and push near the one edge of the strings.

Step by Step Instruction:

1. For the Window Belt, the first knot is connected only with the holding strings. Cross the cord left under the right one.

2. Using the left cord tie a Double Half Hitch in a clockwise direction to your right. So, the knot will be resting beside the tape.

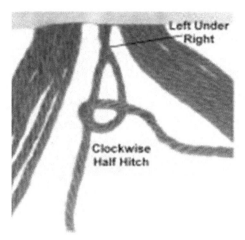

3. Organize the 2 holding strings on the top of working strings diagonally. The angle will be as similar as possible to a 45 degrees' angle.

Useful tip: It is challenging to attach delicate strings so that they remain snug. So use one hand to lead the holding string when you tie the knots with the other. This will allow you to shift the holding cord if necessary in any direction.

In the illustrations below, the holding strings cannot be perfectly straight. They were tilted so that you could easily grasp the knots. Hold the holding strings straight and stiff all the time when doing this project.

In that order, connect working strings 6 to 1 to your holding cord. Ensure that each working string should be pulled straight before tightening each knot. The Half Hitches are now tied in the clockwise direction, as you move from left towards right.

4. In that order, add cords 7 to 12 to your holding cord.

The knots are connected in an anti-clockwise direction, as you move from left to right.

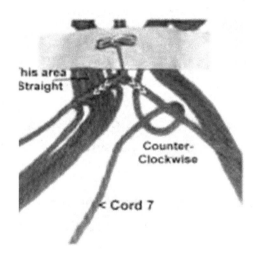

5. To begin the diamonds lower half, shift the left holding string diagonally to the right. Aim to create an angle as similar as possible to a 45 degrees' angle. Organize and keep the working strings straight. Put a small pin at an edge, withholding cord on its outside.

Holding
Cord

6. Locate your working string 6 that is nearest to the midpoint. Flip it over the other strings and heading left. Confirm that it lies under your holding string.

Tie the DHH in the counterclockwise direction, as you move from left towards right. Verify that it lies at a corner against the pin.

Attach cords 5-1 in the same way, each one folding above the others.

After adding a pin at the corner, move the right holding string diagonally to the left side. Attach strings 7 to 12 to the pin with DHH in a clockwise direction, each one folding over the other.

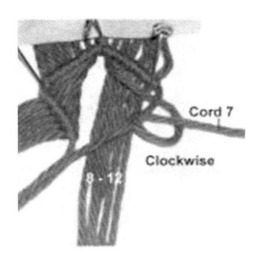

7. To finish a first diamond of the Window Belt, connect the left holding string with a DHH in a clockwise direction to your right holding cord. Drag your finger inside the diamond along the sides of a window to create it look as oval in shape as possible.

8. Repeat steps 2-6, becoming the first half of the permanent diamonds in the Window Belt. Make sure that you match sufficiently to allow 1/2 of the section that you're targeting for. For each diamond in the top half, join cords 6 to 1 and 7 to 12 (in that order) with your holding cords.

Aim to keep the cords straight in the field above the row on which you are working. Once all the pins are withdrawn, this will result in a gentle curve.

Start with cord 6 for the bottom half of each diamond, followed by cords 5-1, folding each over the holding cord at the left side.

Start with the string 7 on the right, then join cords from 8-12.

End the diamond through joining the left holding string to the right side.

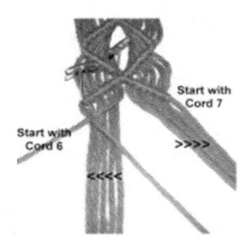

9. When the Window Belt's first half is completed, turn it around entirely and go back to the middle. To do the next half repeat from steps 3-7.

10. Fasten both of the ends of your holding strings by either using an Over-hand or a

Barrel knot. When it's completed, apply glue and break off the extra when dry.

Overhand
or Barrel Knot
with Holding Cords

Now you'll make the braided which ties to shape the closure of your Window Belt. It is the optional step to follow, whether you like to make a particular type of clasp or closure.

11. Arrange the cords in three sets of four working cords and mentally tag them from left towards right. Switch group one to the middle between the two other groups. It must move over and above group 2.

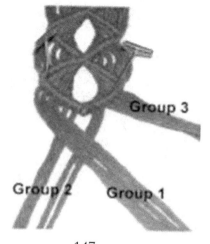

Group 3

Group 2   Group 1

147

12. Now shift group three to the middle, among the two other groups. It will cross over group one.

13. Moves group two to over group three. Now it's in the middle, between the two other groups.

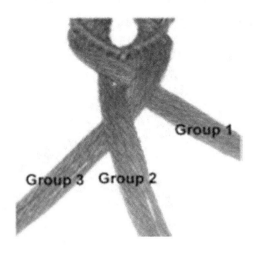

14. Repeat stage 10 to 12 to keep on weaving the tie. Pull as tight as possible, to get it secure at its place. Continue until it becomes 12-15 inches long.

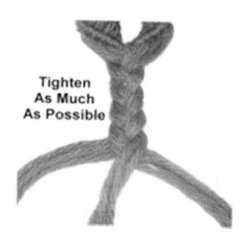

Tighten
As Much
As Possible

15. Use the whole group of strings to form the Overhand knot to protect the braid. Try to get the cords lined neatly. Cut the cords together to create a thin fringe.

Overhand Knot
with Entire Group

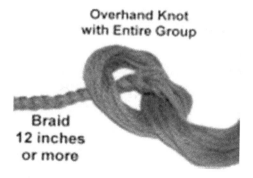

Braid
12 inches
or more

16. At the other end of the Window Belt replicate steps 10-14.

PART III

Chapter 8. Various Objects Project

Double Beaded Macramé Bracelet

Materials List:

• 2m 1mm black waxed cord

• 40cm 2mm black waxed cord

• 60 4-6mm beads (the hole must be at least 1mm wide)

• 1 10-12 flat bead or button (the hole must be central and at least 2mm wide)

• PVA glue

• Clear nail varnish

Tools List:

• Macramé board and Pins (optional)

• Craft knife or sharp pointed scissors

Step 1 - Dip the ends of the 1mm cord into the clear nail varnish. If using superglue add a drop to each end. Allow to dry. This stops the ends of the cord fraying and makes it easier to thread the beads on in the further steps.

Tie and loop in the end of the cord big enough so the flat bead will fit through with some pressure. If the fit is too loose the bracelet may come unfastened. Pin the loop to your macramé board, if using.

Step 2 - Fold the remaining waxed cord in half. This will be used to tie the knots. Place this cord under the length attached to the board and tie one square knot over the cord length and the short end left from creating the loop.

Pull the knot tight.

Step 3 - Thread one bead onto each end of the knotting cord. Push these up the cord until they are resting against the central cord.

Step 4 - Now tie one square knot under the beads. While tying the knot adjust the thread tension and beads as needed so that the beads are touching the central cord.

Step 5 - Repeat steps 4 and 5 until you have added 30 pairs of beads.

Step 6 - Cut off the remaining knotting cords and cover the ends and a small area around them in PVA glue. Do not worry about the glue showing as it will dry clear. Allow the glue to dry until it is at least touch dry.

Step 7 - Thread the button or flat bead on to the central cord and leaving a few millimeters for movement tie a knot to hold it on the cord. Trim off the remaining central cord, leaving a short end. This end can be dipped into clear nail varnish to prevent it from fraying or left as it is.

Endless Falls Macramé Bracelet

Materials List:

• 60cm length of 2mm black waxed cotton cord

• 40-inch length of red waxed cotton cord

• 1 8-10mm flat bead

Tools List:

• Macramé board and Pins (optional)

• Scissors

• Ruler

• PVA glue

Step 1 - Fold the black cord in half and lay it in from of you or pin to your macramé board.

Step 2 - Fold the red cord I half and place the half-way point underneath the black cords.

162

Step 3 - Cross the red cords over the front of the black. It does not matter which cord is on top, but ensure that it is the same in each knot or the pattern will not form correctly.

Step 4 - Pick up the black cords and thread them through the loop formed by the red cords and between the two black cords.

Step 5 - Tighten the knot by pulling the black cords downwards.

Position the knot approximately 1cm below the black cord ends, creating a loop. This loop forms part of the bracelet fastener so needs to be a tight fit for the bead to pass through.

Step 6 - Cross the red cords over the front of the black cords.

Step 7 - Pick up the black cords and thread them through the loop formed by the red cords and between the two black cords.

Step 8 - Pull the black cords downwards to tighten the knot until it rests beneath the first knot.

Step 9 - Repeat steps 6-8 until the bracelet measures 7.5 inches long. Holding all four cords at the cross-over point with one

hand, while threading the black cords with the other is a good technique for tying this type of knot.

Step 10 - Now tie one square knot using the red cords and pull the knot tight.

Step 11 - Cut off the excess red cords and one of the lengths of the black cord.

Step 12 - Cover the cut cord ends and the surrounding area in PVA glue and leave until dry.

Step 13 - Thread the flat bead onto the remaining black cord. Leaving a 3mm gap, tie an overhand knot to secure the bead.

Step 14 - Cut off the remaining cord, leaving a short end. The cord end can be dipped in PVA if desired to stop it from fraying.

Zigzag Bracelet

Materials List:

• 60cm length of 2mm black waxed cotton cord

• 150cm length of 2mm black waxed cotton cord

• 16 8mm oval beads (must have a 2mm hole minimum)

• 1 15mm disk bead or button with central hole (minimum hole diameter of 4mm) Tools List

• Macramé board and Pins (optional)

• Scissors

• Clear nail varnish (optional)

• PVA glue

Step 1 - Fold the shorter length of cord in half and place it around a pin on your macramé board, if using. If not just lay the cord on a flat surface.

Step 2 - Fold the longer length of cord in half and tie one square knot around the shorter cords.

This knot needs to be placed so that the loop created at the end of the shorter cords is a tight fit for the disk bead to fit through.

Step 3 - Tie a further four square knots.

Step 4 - Thread eight beads onto each of the central cords.

Step 5 - Pick up the longer cord on the right and take it across the central cord, under the first bead and then under the central

cords so it come out back on the right side under the first bead on the right side central cord.

Step 6 - Repeat step 5 until you have wrapped the right cord around all the beads, moving the beads into place as you go.

Step 7 - Holding the right cord in place at the bottom of the beads, repeat steps 5 and 6 using the left side longer cord.

Step 8 - Now tie one square knot to secure the wrapped cords.

Step 9 - Tie another four square knots to match the ones at the start of the bracelet.

Step 10 - Cut off the excess length outer cord lengths and cover the ends and surrounding area with PVA glue. The glue will secure the ends and dries clear so will not show. Allow the glue to dry.

Thread the disk bead onto the two central cord and leaving a gap of a few millimeters, tie an overhand knot to secure. After cutting off the excess cord in step 11, the ends can be dipped into clear nail varnish if desired. Once dry, this will stop the cord from fraying.

Chapter 9. More Various Objects Projects - 1

Fringe Earrings

You can reuse old fringes to make earrings. Many garments include fringes as decorative material that you can take advantage of to make your DIY crafts. You can find colored edges on t-shirts, bags, coats, backpacks, or bags of all kinds.

You can recycle colored fringes from clothes you no longer use. Many containers, packs, or T-shirts include these beads.

The exciting thing about making your accessories is to reuse materials and fabrics that you may have forgotten at home. In this way, you contribute to recycling, make responsible consumption, and avoid acquiring unnecessary clothing. If you have fringes, you can also buy them in jewelry bead shops.

Do you prefer to make your fringes? It is effortless, and you need synthetic and resistant thread, contact glue, and scissors.

Make your fringe earrings step by step. You only need contact glue, synthetic yarn, and scissors. To complete the ornaments, you will also need jewelry, caps and earring hooks.

First of all, wrap 3 meters of thread over your fingers, hold it and tie it with more ribbon, cut the threads on the opposite end, use another piece of string and wrap it around the related part, tie it from behind and use glue to fix the knot. Finally, use scissors to cut the excess piece.

At this point, we should already have our two fringes ready to turn them into beautiful earrings. From here, we have several options; the option that we recommend is to use jewelry caps for ornaments and contact glue.

The last step is to use two earring hooks on each cap. You can use jewelry pliers if you need to open and fix the rings or any other material you use.

You can get all the materials used in specialized jewelry stores or by recycling old earrings that you no longer apply.

Crochet Earrings

You can prepare your earrings with the crochet or crochet technique very quickly and with few materials. You will only need a thread of your favorite color, crochet hook, scissors, and two hooks or pieces of earrings.

The only thing you have to master to prepare these earrings is the crochet technique. You have many tutorials on the Internet where they explain how to get started with crocheting.

We recommend making crochet pieces that are about 7 centimeters long at most. If you are not sure which earrings are best for you. Crochet is a simple technique, but requires a little practice.

Once we have our crochet pieces, we can add a bit of transparent glue to make them firmer. The last step is to attach the earring hook. You can use pliers or pliers to tighten the clamp and prevent it from coming loose.

Thread Earrings

We will analyze how to prepare thread earrings step by step. To achieve a different result than the fringe earrings that we have seen in the previous block, we are going to build our thread earrings in the form of thread earrings.

You can develop your thread earrings with the colored threads you like best. You only need a few materials, and the process is straightforward.

To prepare these beautiful earrings, we will only need cotton or synthetic thread, scissors, clips, beads in the shape of booklets, felt, and contact glue.

The first step is to wrap the thread around a rectangular object. Keep in mind that the size of the box or cartridge used must be the size of the earrings that we are going to make

The perfect size would be a matchbox or a cartridge of similar dimensions, but you can use a larger box if you want larger earrings. It is recommended to roll it around 80 or 100 times. Once finished, we cut one side and press the other side to prevent the threads from becoming disordered.

The next step is to cut the threads on the opposite side and join them. Repeat this process for each earring and add as many threads as you see fit.

181

At this point, we will begin to prepare the fastening of the ornaments using the beads in the form of booklets. The first step is to cut some pieces of felt the size of the booklets, as you see in the following image.

Get beads and necessary materials on craft websites or specialty stores in your city. You can also recycle old pieces of jewelry that you don't use.

The next step is to use the contact glue to attach the threads to each part of the felt (one for each earring). You can use tweezers to carry out the process more rigorously. Note that you must glue them on both sides of the felt. If you need more yarn, you can repeat step one as many times as you consider appropriate.

Next, glue the beads in book form with each of the felts. Again, use more contact glue so that they felt adequately adheres. Use tweezers or fine pliers to tighten if you need to.

With this, we will have finished our accessories. The last step is to use earring hooks on the small rings of the golden beads.

Flamenco Earrings

The flamenco earrings that we propose you can easily make with plastic or artificial flowers. Also, you will need some felt, scissors, earring rings, and clear glue.

Optionally, you can use beads or shiny pieces of jewelry.

The plastic flowers are very cheap, and you can buy them in stores decor. You can use the colors that you like best, but we recommend not selecting too large compositions.

Get plastic flowers and the colors you like the most in decoration shops. You can find them at significantly reduced prices. To join them, you only need contact glue and small strips of felt.

The trick to making these earrings is to help you with pieces of felt cut to size and that adhere correctly to the hoops. You can cut pieces of moon-shaped felt and use contact glue, clear glue, or silicone to join the plastic flowers and possible shiny beads.

You must assemble two pieces of felt with flowers of similar size or as identical as possible so that the earrings are symmetrical. The key is to join the two pieces on both sides of the ring so that they are entirely symmetrical (identical on both sides).

In total, you must prepare four pieces of felt with flowers (two for each hoop earring).

With The Macramé Technique

We prefer the simplest, most minimalist, medium-sized macramé elaborations. But for tastes, there are colors! Do you prefer more complex and extensive elaborations? No problem!

You can create hoop macramé earrings or with a simple hook, as you like. Use different colors and shapes to create something more personalized.

In the case of macramé earrings in the form of a hoop, you must join your piece with a part of the circle so that the macramé is a continuation of it. In the case of using a regular earring hook, you must leave a small hole in your macramé to place a hoop and on this the hook.

We prefer minimalist and symmetrical earrings, but you can vary the color in each earring. If you are more daring, you can even change the shape or size.

Chapter 10. More Various Objects Projects - 2

In case you're searching for some amateur neighborly macramé project ideas, you've come to the ideal place!

I need to impart to you different macramé project ideas you can make. I will likely assist you with taking advantage of your inward imaginative potential and assist you with making wonderful macramé artwork pieces you can impart to the world.

In case you're new to the world of macramé, or maybe, you have just been familiar with it. Now you need to get again into the section of things, I have made a wide range of macramé extends all through my macramé journey, and I will be sharing a portion of the past macramé projects I have made, to ideally assist you with drawing motivation so you can start to make your own.

I have cover out a couple of various designs and activities I trust you should begin making before proceeding onward to more many-sided structures and further developed macramé pieces.

For the present, we should kick you off on the right foot in learning some novice cordial DIY macramé projects!

When you finish, ideally, you've picked up the conviction and certainty that you can do this. It would be up to you and your creative mind with what you might want to make. How about we start!

Macramé Keychain

When you are open to making the fundamental macramé ties, you will probably need to bounce in and start on a task immediately.

For the primary macramé project thought, we will begin with a basic and simple macramé key chain. A macramé key chain is an extraordinary place to start since it requires an insignificant string, supplies, and time to make.

I started my macramé project by making key chains. I needed to figure out knotting the knots and accepted that beginning with smaller activities would be an incredible method to get me there. Making key chains showed me how to tie various knots by practicing and repeating different knots and how to join different frills, for example, beads and pearls into my activities. The best part about this specific task was that once finished, and I had the option to put it to utilize myself or give it as a blessing.

If you are keen on figuring out how to make macramé key chains, at that point, this beginner benevolent DIY project might be directly for you. It very well may be finished in an hour, relying upon your expertise level. In this example, the principal takeaway is getting yourself acquainted with macramé hitches and working on knotting methods.

The following are the provisions and the lengths of string required for this project. Track with the YouTube video instructional exercise to get the bit by bit process on the best way to assemble the key chain.

Macramé Supplies Needed:

- Turn-Key hanger
- 3mm Single Strand Cord or 3/4 Ply Cord
- 6 x 5mm Gap Beads
- Lengths of Cord Needed:
- 1 x 90cm
- 4 x 100cm

Macramé Flower Vase Hanger

A follow-up to the macramé key chain is a macramé flower jar hanger project.

In case you're in any way similar to me and appreciate the fragrance of new flowers, you'll unquestionably appreciate making a macramé container hanger you can place your flowers in after.

Like the macramé key chain, this macramé flower container hanger doesn't expect you to utilize various knots. The knots utilized for this project will be your fundamental Square knot and Double Half Knot tie.

The main difficulty you may discover with this task will locate the fitting container size to macramé for this project. It isn't vital to utilize precisely the same size of the container we've recorded and relied upon what you decide to utilize, and you can modify your cord lengths in like manner. Other than that, a macramé jar hanger will be genuinely straight forward and simple to make.

This task is evaluated to take around 60 minutes. Contingent upon the size and state of your container, the time will vary.

When you have finished creating a macramé flower container hanger, you'll have a dazzling macramé piece you can put on a lounge area table, side table, or shelf.

Macramé Supplies Needed:

- Flower Vase
- 3mm Cotton Cord
- Line Lengths:
- 18 x 155"
- 2 x 18"

Macramé Tassel Earring

The most effective method to make macramé tassel earrings

We're currently getting into one of my preferred macramé projects – hoops! All the more explicitly, tassel hoops.

In case you're hoping to get some motivation and ideas for your next macramé project, look no further as macramé earrings are an incredible apprentice amicable project you can rapidly begin with.

Macramé earrings are easy to make and are ideal for any event. You can wear them as a fashion statement, blending and coordinating with different accessories. It is a great method to show your exceptional style and artistry – I appreciate making macramé earrings, therefore.

For this macramé project, you will spend around 45 min – 1 hour to make them. You will utilize just two knots for this project – a twofold half knot tie an overhand tie. You will no doubt need to get yourself some macramé string and a couple of band earrings for this project.

If earrings interest you, be certain you give this macramé DIY project a go!

Macramé Materials Needed:

- 3mm Cotton Cord
- Weaving String
- Earrings
- Length of Cotton Cord:
- 6 x (3" – 5") threads (for one hoop)
- Length of Embroidery String:
- 1 x 22" (for one earring)

Macramé Coaster

Hoping to add some DIY home, stylistic theme to your living space? Have a go at making this adorable little macramé coaster!

Macramé coaster is an extraordinary beginner DIY project for anybody hoping to begin on their first barely any macramé projects. This project will fill you 2 needs.

1. Help invigorate your imagination and;

2. It is reasonable and can be utilized.

This is an incredible macramé project thought in case you're hoping to make something reasonably without any problem. It's superb for those hoping to begin with macramé or the individuals who simply need to make some macramé liners.

As a heads up, in case you're anticipating causing this napkin, to know it can get somewhat dubious with regards to knotting and knotting in a round shape. You will discover when working in a circular shape, and you will frequently be required to continually turn and move the project around the task while you are knotting. It can get somewhat befuddling on occasion, yet with some training; you ought to have the option to easily float through the creation of these liners in a matter of moments.

For this task, you may be required to know 2 knots – the lark's head knot and twofold half knot tie. The estimated time for this project is 60 minutes.

Macramé Materials Needed:

- 4mm Single Strand Cotton Cord
- Stitch Hook
- Lengths of Cord
- 3 x 170cm 1 x 50cm

Macramé Feathers

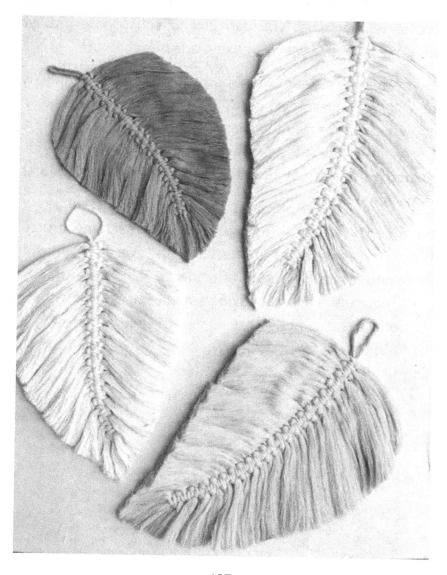

If you're hoping to improve your macramé projects with more details and texture, there's no preferred path over by including feathers. You can likewise transform the feathers into straightforward key chains, hoops, charms or other jewelry also.

For this fledgling DIY macramé project, I will share three contrast macramé feathers that you can use to consolidate into your greater macramé projects or make it a feather charm.

Macramé feathers stand apart because of its fluffy fringe and texture. It's troublesome not to stop and take a second look when you see a macramé project brightened with feathers and leaves. Many respects the feathers and leaves on a piece and are fascinated to figure out how to make them sooner or later in their macramé project.

If you're hoping to say something with your macramé structures and projects, there's no preferred path over with macramé feathers and leaves. To figure out how to make these feathers, you will require the accompanying supplies and track within the instructional exercise beneath. Feel free to check it out!

Macramé Supplies Needed:

- 4mm Single Strand Cotton Cord
- Treated steel brush
- Estimating Tape
- Lengths of Cord:
- Feathers #1 (11cm wide, 14cm height)
- 1 x 40cm Strand
- 14 x (13-15cm) Strands
- Feathers Tassel #2 (11cm wide, 14cm height)
- 1 x 90cm Strand
- 1 x 150cm Strand
- 14 x (13-15cm) Strand
- Feathers #3 (11cm wide, 14cm height)
- 1 x 30cm Strand
- 1 x 80cm Strand
- 8 x (13-15cm) Strand

Macramé Mason Jar Plant Hanger

How to make a macramé Mason jar holder

When you have finished a couple of little macramé projects, it's presently time to gradually turn up the dial on your macramé abilities. This project is an incredible Segway into figuring out how to make a medium measured macramé.

Practically indistinguishable from a macramé plant hanger, macramé artisan container hangers are intended to hang smaller family unit improvements, for example, candles, desert plants, sweets, and every other kind of smaller book.

This macramé project thought is extraordinary for anybody hoping to improve their macramé abilities and will require more cord than your smaller estimated macramé projects. You will be taking a look at around 1 – 2 hours to finish this task and will utilize 6 sorts of knots. – Lark's head tie, berry tie, twofold half knot tie, square knot, group tie.

At the point when you begin getting into medium/bigger measured macramé extends, it's ideal to see what number of threads and length of each line you will require for the project. A general guideline that I like to utilize is to increase the surmised length of your task by 4 to get the line length you need to work with. Likewise, you will need to duplicate that number by 2 if you are collapsing the string into equal parts and connecting it onto a dowel/ring, utilizing a lark's head knot.

Macramé Materials Needed:

- 3mm Single Strand Cotton Cord
- Little wooden ring or metal ring
- Scissors
- Estimating Tape
- Length of Cord:
- 6 x 200cm
- 1 x 30cm

Chapter 11. More Various Objects Projects - 3

Pendant

Create a pendant! Beaded cord is attached to your finished micro-Macramé centerpiece. Tropical lagoon colors combine to create the ebb and flow of this project. Anchoring things together is a lobster clasp. The finished length, stem to stern, is 10 inches. Cast off your cares and enjoy smooth sailing with this design!

Knots Used:

- Verticle Lark's Head Knot

- Flat Knot

- Half-Hitch Knot

Supplies:

- Blush C-Lon cord, 6 ft. cord (x4), 2 1/2 ft. cord (x1), 1 ft. cord (x2)

- 12mm Teal beads (x5)

- 8mm Tan beads (x8)

- Size 11 seed beads, teal (x14)

- 2.5mm Gold Crimp beads (x2)

- Size 6 seed beads, assorted teal and bronze (x133)

- 2mm Gold crimp beads (x2)

- Antique gold leaves, about 1mm (x3)

- Gold lobster clasp and jump ring

- Large gold crimp bead (U-shaped, might be labeled for leather cord) (x2)

- Glue - Beacon 527 multi-use

Instructions:

1. Place 4 cords through the ring at the top of an end crimp clasp. Fold the cords in half, for a total of 8 cords. Lay the cords in the crimp; glue and crimp shut. Turnover.

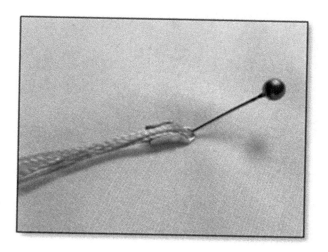

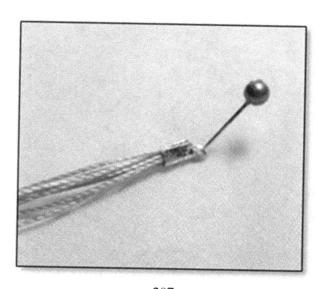

Tie a flat knot with outer 2 cords around all others.

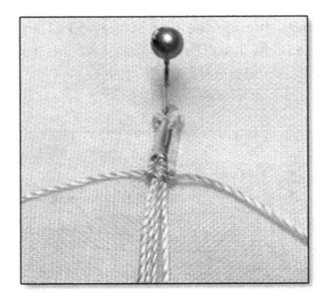

2. Separate 3-3-2.   With the left 3: Find the left cord and tie 7 Vertical Lark's Head (VLH) knots around the other 2 cords.

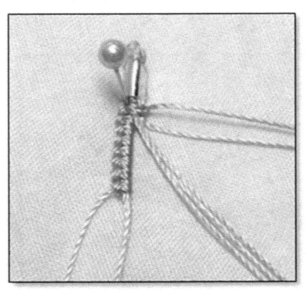

3. With the center 3: Find the left cord and tie 3 VLH knots around the other 2 cords.

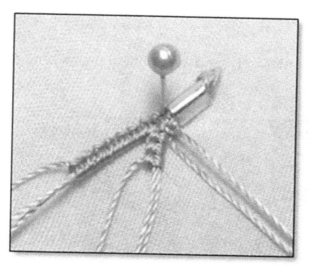

4. Place all 6 cords together. Bend the left section outwards, then take the left cord and tie a VLH knot around the other 5 cords. NOTE: tighten up each section as you attach them together.

5. With the left 3: Find the left cord and tie 5 VLH knots around the other 2 cords.

6. With the center 3: Thread a size 6 teal beads onto all 3 cords.

7. Place the left 6 cords together. Arc the left section outwards, then take the left cord and tie a VLH knot around the other 5 cords. (NOTE: tighten up each section as you attach them together).

8. With the left 3: Find the left cord and tie 7 VLH knots around the other 2 cords.

9. With the center 3: Find the left cord and tie 3 VLH knots around the other 2 cords.

10. Place these 6 cords together. Arc the left section outwards, then take the left cord and tie a VLH knot around the other 5 cords. (Remember to tighten things up). Set aside this section.

11. Using the right 2 cords: With the outer cord, tie 3 VLH knots onto the inner cord, then place a seed bead onto the outer cord. Tie 2 VLH knots, and then place a seed bead onto the outer cord. Tie 2 VLH knots with the outer cord, then put a seed bead onto the outer cord and tie 3 VLH knots.

Place all 8 cords together and find the left cord. Use it to tie a VLH knot around all others.

12. Repeat steps 2 to 11 to create the second section. Note: when starting the second section, move one of the longer cords to the outside to use as the knotting cord. You won't be able to tell that you snuck it over there.

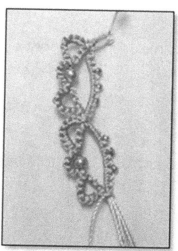

Center Section

13. Separate cords 2-2-3-1. Find the right cord and thread on a bronze size 6 bead, a 12mm teal bead and another bronze size 6 bead. Set aside.

14. Find the right 3 cords. Using the right cord as the wrapping cord (WC), tie half hitch (HH) knots to create a bundle 3 ½ cm long. Set aside.

15. With the center 2 cords: Move the longest cord to the left and use as the WC. Tie 9 VLH knots.

16. With left 2: Move the longer cord to the left to use as the WC. Tie 13 VLH knots.

17. Put the 4 left cords together and tie a VLH knot with the left cord. Place 3 size 6 beads on the right 2 cords (teal, gold, and teal).

18. With the left 2: Tie 8 VLH knots. Put the 4 cords together and tie a VLH knot with the left cord.

19. With left 2, tie 13 VLH knots. With right 2, tie 9 VLH knots. Place the 4 cords together and tie a VLH knot with the left cord.

Put all 8 cords together and tie a VLH knot with the left cord. (End of Center Section)

20. Repeat steps 2 through 11 twice. Note: Tighten up the right 2 cords before working with them. If you start with the right cords here it will lock things in place.

Turn the piece over and place the cords in the large crimp bead. Glue in place and crimp shut. Trim the ends.

Finishing

1. Place together the 2 ½ ft. cord and one of the 1 ft. cords, keeping the longer cord on the right. Thread them through the 2.5mm crimp bead, the lobster clasp and back through the crimp bead. Crimp the crimp bead.

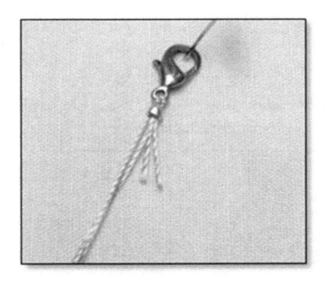

2. Bead as follows: (Note: when beading be careful to keep the longer cord on the right at all times. If the cords get twisted inside the beads, it will skew the design).

3. Onto both cords; 1 dark teal, 1 frosted teal, 1 teal, 1 light copper, 1 dark copper, 1 light copper, 1 teal, 1 frosted teal, 1 dark teal followed by an 8mm tan bead. Repeat 3 times.

4. Place on cords 1 dark teal, 1 frosted teal, 1 teal, 1 light copper, 1 dark copper, and 1 light copper. Now separate the cords, with the longest cord to the right.

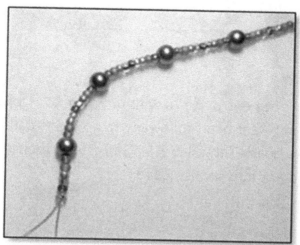

5. Onto the left cord only place 1 teal, 1 frosted teal, 1 dark teal, 1 light copper, 1 dark copper, 1 light copper, then 1 dark teal, 1 frosted teal, and 1 teal. Now attach this cord to the pendant with a 2mm crimp bead.

6. Onto the right cord place: 1 dark teal, 1 gold, 1 bronze bead. Then the 12mm teal bead followed by gold, 2 frosted teal, and another gold bead. Thread on a 12mm teal, then a bronze, 2 dark teal, and another bronze bead.

7. Put on a gold leaf, a size 11 teal seed bead, and repeat that once more, then follow up with a third gold leaf.

8. Continue beading with a bronze, 2 dark teal, and another bronze bead followed by the 12mm teal bead. A size 6 gold, 2 frosted teal and another gold bead go on next, then the last 12mm teal bead. Now 1 bronze, 1 gold and 1 dark teal.

9. Tighten up the beading. Take the remaining 1 ft. cord and attach it to the right side of the pendant with a 2mm crimp bead.

10. Continue beading as shown – matching the first side (remember to keep the cords parallel inside the beads).

11.Thread both cords through the 2.5mm crimp bead, then through the jump ring and back through the crimp bead.

12. Tighten up the beading then crimp the crimp bead. Glue and trim.

Chapter 12. More Various Objects Projects - 4

Serenity Bracelet

(**Note:** if you are familiar with the flat knot, you can move right along into the next pattern)

This novice bracelet offers plenty of practice using one of micro macramé's most used knots. You will also gain experience in beading and equalizing tension. This bracelet features a button closure and the finished length is 7 inches.

Flat Knot (aka square knot)

Overhand knot

Materials:

- White C-Lon cord, 6 ½ ft., x 3
- 18 - Frosted Purple size 6 beads
- 36 - Purple seed beads, size 11
- 1 - 1 cm Purple and white focal bead
- 26 - Dark Purple size 6 beads
- 1 - 5 mm Purple button closure bead

(**Note:** the button bead needs to be able to fit into all 6 cords)

Take all 3 cords and fold them in half. Find the center and place on your work surface as shown:

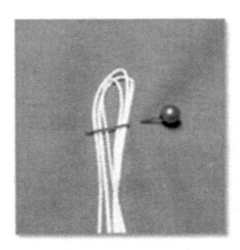

Now hold the cords and tie an overhand knot, loosely, at the center point. It should look like this:

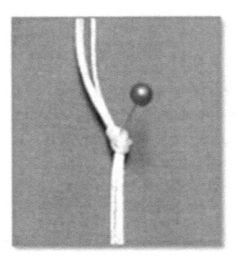

1. We will now make a buttonhole closure. Just below the knot, take each outer cord and tie a flat knot (aka square knot). Continue tying flat knots until you have about 2 ½ cm.

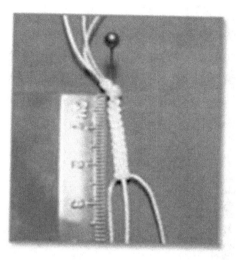

2. Undo your overhand knot and place the ends together in a horseshoe shape.

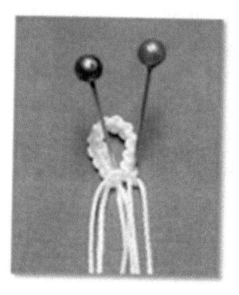

3. We now have all 6 cords together. Think of the cords as numbered 1 through 6 from left to right. Cords 2-5 will stay in the middle as filler cords. Find cord 1 and 6 and use these to tie flat knots around the filler cords. (Note: now you can pass your button bead through the opening to ensure a good fit. Add or subtract flat knots as needed to create a snug fit. This size should be fine for a 5mm bead). Continue to tie flat knots until you have 4 cm worth. (To increase bracelet length, add more flat knots here and the equal amount in step 10).

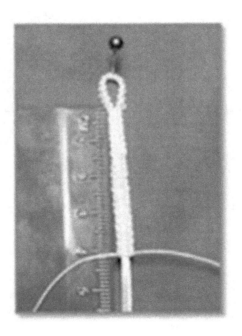

4. Separate cords 1-4-1. Find the center 2 cords. Thread a size 6 frosted purple bead onto them, then tie a flat knot with cords 2 and 5.

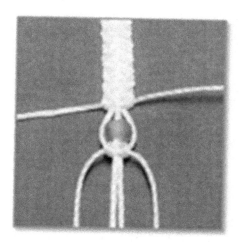

5. We will now work with cords 1 and 6. With cord 1, thread on a seed bead, a dark purple size 6 beads and another seed bead. Repeat with cord 6, and then separate the cords into 3-3. Tie a flat knot with the left 3 cords. Tie a flat knot with the right 3 cords.

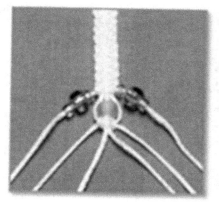 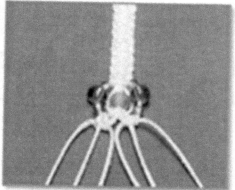

6. Repeat step 4 and 5 three times.

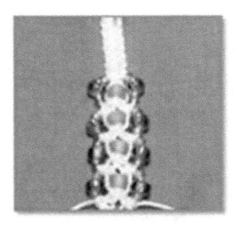

7. Find the center 2 cords, hold together and thread on the 1cm focal bead. Take the next cords out (2 and 5) and bead as follows: 2 size 6 dark purple beads, a frosted purple bead, and 2 dark purple beads. Find cords 1 and 6 and bead as follows: 2 frosted purple beads, a seed bead, a dark purple bead, a seed bead, 2 frosted purple beads.

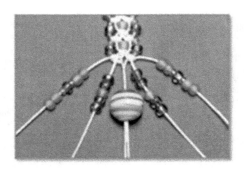

8. With cords 2 and 5, tie a flat knot around the center 2 cords. Place the center 4 cords together and tie a flat knot around them with outer cords 1 and 6.

9. Repeat steps 4 and 5 four times.

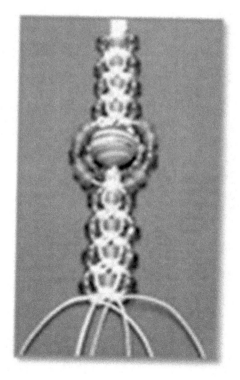

10. Repeat step 3.

11. Place your button bead on all 6 cords and tie an overhand knot tight against the bead. Glue well and trim the cords.

Lantern Bracelet

This pattern may look simple, but please don't try it if you are in a hurry. This one takes patience. Don't worry about getting your picot knots all the exact same shape. Have fun with it! The finished bracelet is 7 ¼ inches in length. If desired, add a picot knot and a spiral knot on each side of the centerpiece to lengthen it. This pattern has a jump ring closure.

Spiral Knot

Picot Knot

Overhand Knot

Materials:

- 3 strands of C-Lon cord (2 light brown and 1 medium brown) 63-inch lengths
- Fasteners (1 jump ring, 1 spring ring or lobster clasp)
- 8 small beads (about 4mm) amber to gold colors
- 30 gold seed beads
- 3 beads (about 6 mm) amber color (mine are rectangular, but round or oval will work wonderfully also)

Note: Bead size can vary slightly. Just be sure all beads you choose will slide onto 2 cords (except seed beads).

1. Find the center of your cord and attach it to the jump ring with a knot. Repeat with the 2 remaining strands. If you want the 2-tone effect, be sure your second color is NOT placed in the center, or it will only be a filler cord and you will end up with a 1 tone bracelet.

2. You now have 6 cords to work with. Think of them as number 1 to 6, from left to right. Move cords 1 and 6 apart from the rest. You will use these to work the spiral knot. All others are filler cords. Take cord number 1 and tie a spiral knot. Always begin with the left cord. Tie 7 more spirals.

3. Place a 4mm bead on the center 2 cords. Leave cords 1 and 6 alone for now and work 1 flat knot using cords 2 and 5.

4. Now put cords 2 and 5 together with the center strands. Use 1 and 6 to tie a picot flat knot. If you don't like the look of your picot knot, loosen it up and try again. Gently tug the cords into place, then lock in tightly with the next spiral knot.

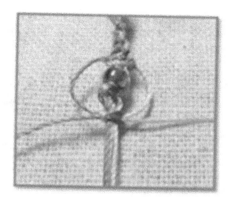

Notice here how I am holding the picot knot with my thumbs while pulling the cords tight with my fingers. If you look closely you may be able to see that I have a cord in each hand.

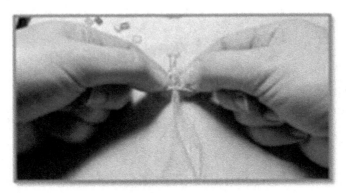

5. Tie 8 spiral knots (using left cord throughout pattern).

6. Place a 4mm bead on the center 2 cords. Leave cords 1 and 6 alone for now and work 1 flat knot using cords 2 and 5. Now put cords 2 and 5 together with the center strands. Use strands 1 and 6 to tie a picot flat knot.

7. Repeat steps 5 and 6 until you have 5 sets of spirals.

8. Next place 5 seed beads on cords 1 and 6. Put cords 3 and 4 together and string on a 6 mm bead. Tie one flat knot with the outermost cords.

Repeat this step two more times.

Now repeat steps 5 and 6 until you have 5 sets of spirals from the center point. Thread on your clasp. Tie an overhand knot with each cord and glue well. Let dry completely. As this is the weakest point in the design, I advise trimming the excess cords and gluing again. Let dry.

Celtic Choker

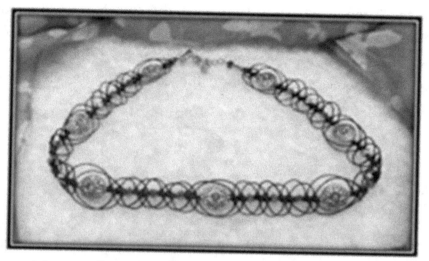

Elegant loops allow the emerald and silver beads to stand out, making this a striking piece. The finished length is 12 inches. Be sure to use the ribbon clasp which gives multiple length options to the closure.

Alternating Lark's Head Chain

Materials:

- 3 strands of black C-Lon cord; two 7ft cords, one 4ft cord
- 18 - Green beads (4mm)
- 7 - Round silver beads (10 mm)
- Fasteners: Ribbon Clasps, silver

Note: Bead size can vary slightly. Just be sure all beads you choose will slide onto 2 cords.

1. Optional – Find the center of your cord and attach it to the top of the ribbon clasp with a knot. I found it easier to thread the loose ends through and pull them down until my loop was near the opening, then push the cords through the loop. Repeat with the 2 remaining strands, putting the four-foot cord in the center. If this is problematic, you could cut all the cords to 7ft and not worry about placement. (If you really trust your glue, you can skip this step by gluing the cords into the clasp and going from there).

2. Lay all cords into the ribbon clasp. Add a generous dap of glue and use pliers to close the clasp.

3. You now have 6 cords to work with. Find the 4 ft. cords and place them in the center. They will be the holding (or filler) cords throughout.

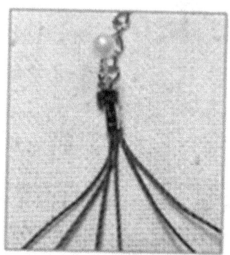

4. Begin your Alternating Lark's Head (ALH) chain, using the outmost right cord then the outermost left cord. Follow with the other right cord, then the last left cord. For this first set, the pattern will be hard to see. You may need to tug gently on the cords to get a little slack in them.

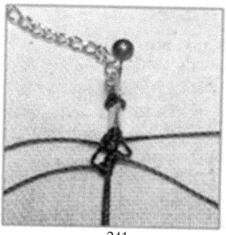

5. Now slide a silver bead onto the center 2 cords.

6. The outer cords are now staggered on your holding cords. Continue with the ALH chain by knotting with the upper right cord...

Then tie a knot with the upper left cord.

7. Finish your set of 4 knots, and then add a green bead

8. Tie four ALH knots followed by a green bead until you have 3 green beads in the pattern. Then tie one more set of 4 ALH knots.

9. Slide on a silver bead and continue creating sequences of 3 green, 1 silver (always with 4 ALH knots between each). End with the 7th silver bead and 1 more set of 4 ALH knots, for a 12" necklace.

10. Lay all cords in the ribbon clasp and glue well.

11. Crimp shut and let dry completely. Trim excess cords.

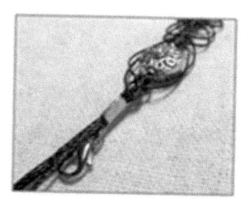

Climbing Vine Keychain

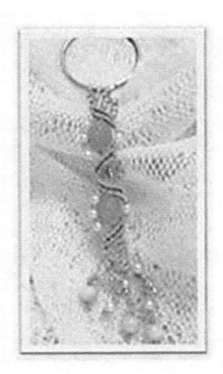

This pattern is a fun way to practice the Diagonal Double Half-Hitch knot. It works up quickly and is a fun piece to work in various colors. Just be sure to use enough beads on the fringe work to weigh the threads down.

Lark's Head

Flat Knot

Diagonal Double Half-Hitch

Materials:

- Measure out 3 cords of Peridot C-Lon, 30" each
- 1 key ring
- 2 (5mm) beads
- 8 (plus extra for the ends) pink seed beads
- 4 (plus extra for the ends) gold seed beads
- 12 (plus extra for the ends) green seed beads
- 8 (plus extra for the ends) 3mm pearl beads (seed pearl beads will work also)

Note: You can vary slightly to the bead size. Just be sure that 2 cords will fit through the 2 main beads (the 5mm size beads)

1.   Fold each cord in half and use to attach it to the key ring. Secure onto your work surface with straight pins. You now have 6 cords to work with.

2. Separate cords into 3 and 3. Using the left 3 cords, tie 2 flat knots. Repeat with the right 3 cords.

Chapter 13. More Various Objects Projects - 5

Barefoot sandals: They are fun projects and are perfect for walking on lawns or grasses in summer or around the beach.

This project is almost, if not the simplest, to make. It's a great way to use up leftover beads and yarn/cord plus it gives the feet a really pretty look. It features one of the most used knots, square knot and another technique of making creative pieces, braiding

Tools to be used:

• Pure cotton yarn or macramé cord

• Scissors

• Large hole beads, for instance: The silver spacer beads.

• The Bulldog clips.

• Knots used:

• Square Knots (SK)

• Braiding

Steps:

1. Make 3 pieces of yarn or cords about 3m long then locate the middle point of the strips and make a knot. It's important the yarn is long; it will be needed for the ankle straps.

2. On one of the sides of the knot, braid strands of 2-3 inches together.

3. Loose the knot which was earlier made, and tie it again once you've made a spiral loop along with the strand that is braided. This creates what is called a toe loop of your sandal!

4. The major sandal part, which goes down from the ankle, to cross the foot's front and then towards the toe, generally, is made using square knots. There are half a dozen strands to use now, so, divide them into 3 strands, with each having two strands.

5. From the right side, put that strand on top of the one in the middle, making D-shaped looking loop. The strand located on the left should be threaded underneath the one in the middle and inside the loop with D-shape.

To make or create the leading section of the square knot, pull the right and the left strands. In the opposite direction, do the same thing for the left side. Move the strand on the left side over the one in the center, and then thread the strand on the right-hand side under the one in the center and backwards into the D-shaped loop. Draw the strands on the right and on the left from the one in the middle to finish the first square knot.

6. Make two other square knots, in addition to the first square knots tied. Next, thread the round beads made of silver on the strand in the center. Then around this same bead, begin the initial part of the next SK.

7. Repeat steps 6 and 7, there should be a total 10 beads, which would be joined to the center strand with macramé SK. A few more beads are needed for bigger sizes).

8. Complete the section with beads by making 1 or 2 plain SK that have no heads and separate the strands in two with each split have about 3 heads. Braid the strands to form the straps for the ankle, till a length/diameter of about 50 centimeters is reached. This will allow you to wrap them round your ankles a few times. Alternatively, another bead made of silver can be added towards the end between a SK for some decoration. When doing this, it is important to make two knots (double knots) towards the bottom part of the final square knot so as to make it firm. Cut off any remaining unused thread and repeat the steps above to make the sandal's second leg.

Chapter 14. The Art of Macramé

For Men and Women who'd like to Grasp How-to Macramé, There's a range of areas available on the marketplace. Creating complex knots that produce whole patterns that could likewise be transformed to exquisite bracelets, flower baskets and decorative wall-hangings is just what Macramé is based on being an art. The exact first and elaborate step in looking to understand just how exactly to Macramé, in case that you're interested in this subject, is understanding how the basic knots and a couple of diagrams.

Visual skills are of immense Assistance and certainly will create learning just how-to Macramé hassle-free. For a lot of people, it's a fantastic deal simpler to follow along with diagrams in the place of written guidelines which may be quite tricky to comprehend. Whenever you've familiarized yourself using the visual assistance, it's the perfect time to acquire the apparatus to initiate the procedure for Macramé.

Beginner Macramé

Just like anything in life you will encounter an Endless amount of techniques to start analyzing a new craft or craft. I am not likely to claim for an expert on Macramé. In fact, I'm an entire newbie. From inch new-comer into still another I'll simply take you throughout my private journey to demonstrate one method to execute it.

I shall provide each of the instruments which you need to find that your Solution to make the enjoyable art of Macramé. The good thing is you do not have to develop into professional to create definitely amazing decoration bits for your dwelling. Frankly, it seems much tougher as its. Thus, let us enter it.

First: Exercise exactly the ideal method to make Macramé

Why should the proceedings that you exercise? Like anything that endeavor is exactly about to price you a tiny bit. Exactly how much? My first 'real' job cost me around $30 because of the Macramé rope (and sometimes even Macramé cord, since it may possibly be understood) and a few dollars because of its very own wooden dowel.

Macramé Practice job

Reasons why I urge a Little "clinic" job:

- It fills the time gap as you wait patiently the Macramé rope.
- This will give you the Opportunity to get familiar with Different Macramé knots, their own titles and the way to complete them.
- By the conclusion of your clinic effort you are going to Be Joyful and totally eager to go bigger or you're getting to see this isn't for you personally.
- Completing this clinic effort will provide you precisely the Assurance to commit your cash and time to choose the subsequent step into to a first "real" Macramé undertaking.

Next: Exactly what Macramé job can I make?

Make a determination concerning exactly what job you may Need to create. Look over pictures of Macramé on the Web. It's possible to hunt Etsy, Pinterest, along with google. Do some researching to master everything exactly is available on the marketplace.

What sorts of Macramé activities will I produce? Start small.

- Plant holder
- Jewelry such as choker necklaces or bracelets
- Wall-hanging
- Novel markers
- Key string
- Bigger jobs comprise:

- Dining table
- Hammock (rescue a significant job such as this for later)
- Lighting-fixture
- Carpet
- Headboard
- Garland or bunting

Choose the job type. Wall-hangings and plant Holders will most likely be both common new-comer tasks.

Where's it planning to move? This can definitely help determine what dimensions you are attempting to produce.

Locate a design which that suits you. Longer free form and organic or symmetric with traces which can be fresh and readily defined patterns?

Where Can I locate Macramé patterns?

Whenever you have determined what Sort of job and Design attracts you personally, you are all set to search for a design. I came across my regimen Esty for under 5.

You don't need to get a design. You will find a Gazillion YouTube pictures that could assist you through construction many tasks that you may possibly undoubtedly love. Three Chief reasons I decided to get a blueprint would be:

I had been searching through Esty for suggestions for what Kind of Project I desired to produce and realized at the point that buying patterns was an alternative. I fell in love with the work that is been precisely what I'd been imaging.

Patterns are a really inexpensive choice ($5-$10).

I enjoyed the idea of not having to work side by Side working with an image, stopping and starting it frequently. Getting off in my own computer seemed more relaxing for me.

What Stuff Do I need For Macramé?

Once you have your own project/pattern you're going to know exactly how much rope to purchase. I presumed that I had to utilize organic cotton collection; however, it's likely to let your personal taste and design show you as you choose your shade & stuff. They promote rope (or cable) around Esty. But, it had been inaccessible at the price or number I desired. Adhering to a great deal of hunting this is the connection which I used.

Can I achieve this?

Yes, I am here to let you know can.

Here's a Very Small Behind the scenes confessional of my own experience:

How Often Could It Choose To Learn That A Macramé Knot?

Inside my clinic endeavor, I lost track of this amount of times I had to repeat the movie into the beginning and begin. And that

I'd have moments after I wondered whether that really was because of me personally. Because of this, it's completely normal to become momentary doubts together side your learning curve.

Selections for the Macramé project if you operate

Under supplies I recorded "rolling clothes Stand" this really is exactly what I used and that was advocated, however, it's costly and maybe not mandatory for those who never had one.

You can work together with your dowel or ring Wrapped out of anywhere that's suitable.

You can hang it in a Door Knob, a drawer, or even anyplace you'll observe to secure your own piece.

Other thoughts would be to use a more suction cup hook or maybe an over-the-door wreath hanger.

You may Defeat a piece of artwork hanging out your walls (temporarily) and hold your bit by the nail.

Assessing outside a diagram, nevertheless well Methodical and clarified that it will likely soon be, won't provide you plenty of assistance to allow you in order to Macramé precisely. It's crucial to find ribbon to have the capability to Macramé effectively. Like some other gained art, attempting to understand just how exactly to Macramé in addition calls for training. Obtain some clear, training samples of diagrams that are simple to secure started. You may quickly realize the ones that are simpler to eventually become simpler compared to the intricacies of the ones that are elaborate. You will manage to progress for them with a great deal of exercise and time.

Macramé is your historic craft of knotting rope or fiber Out of distinct patterns to generate decorative and practical services and products. As much early cultures had depicted linking art and techniques styles, the form of Macramé we utilize every single day has its own roots in ancient china. The saying Macramé is in origin, also suggests 'fringe'.

Over the time period, Macramé disperse through the duration of the orient and Europe, thanks partly to both sailors and sea faring merchants, that practiced the art of knot tying for decorative and endurance purposes. Macramé methods were being used from the dark ages to manage mourning jewelry in the own hair, a practice that lasted into the 19th century. From the Victorian age, Macramé was quite a favorite and stylish pastime in England, used for lace, lace, lace, decorative details, and clothing.

The 1960's and 1970's saw a resurgence of attention in Knotted crafts, together with Macramé plant figurines, wall-hangings, accessories, and jewelry. Vibrant colors and bold designs are part of this minute.

Macramé turns in a sudden Range of design and dwelling accessory items out available now. From hemp jewelry to woven bag bags, Macramé has generated a primary effect on tendency and also at your home. Now's Macramé features thicker, most calming colors and also a more impressive variety of fibers, textures and antiques. Macramé is actually only a fantastic craft--what you'll need can be just a length of cable, a group of scissors, hooks, along with a function coating, therefore it stores and journeys well.

Besides the basic knot patterns you may additionally have in order to exercise and focus for just a little before you'll memorize the activities and also create balanced knots. This won't be heard in case you are in a rush; you have to take actions by measure as a way to grasp just how exactly to Macramé. At any time, you have mastered the very simple knot layouts, and then move up them to generate simple works such as bracelets. Besides the knots, you then must acquire an eye to coincide with the best colorings to supply the knot out works.

Bracelets are Fantastic for Newbies because the easiest Knots are required without a high volume of elegance. If you feel at ease with your skill, then you are able to manage very complex routines. The absolute best confident about complex and incredibly complex designs is they are sometimes completely shaped to generate decorative items which seem very outstanding.

First, choose a time period that would need to fully grasp the way exactly to Macramé would depend upon several variables like how fast you are able position to comprehend the process. If you are knitting or sewing to receive yourself a protracted period, the amount of sophistication needs to be since there really are a few similarities with the practice.

Macramé is a popular way to decorate for decades, Bringing warmth and texture in to a house or apartment with knots that may be placed together in identifying methods of making one-of-a-kind wall hangings, plant holders, and more.

It's Easy to understand the way to Macramé because you simply should understand a handful knots to get paid a Macramé task.

Obtaining studying to knot

Before you are ready to Begin learning the way to Macramé, Gather your gear and familiarize yourself with a few regular Macramé requirements you will need to grasp.

Provides and substances

Here's what you are going to have to know and workout your own Macramé knots:

Macramé cable: that can be Any Type of cord, Twine, or strand made from cotton, jute, or synthetic substance. It arrives in various sizes, colors, and spins. Within this tutorial we found that a 3/16" cotton string provided that rope to acquire clotheslines.

Service: You could require something to link to. Popular Choices comprise dowel sticks, branches, hoops, or bands. We used a dowel rod for all these knots.

Conclusion

There you have it, well done, everything you need to know to get you started with your own macramé knots. You just learned how easy it is to get started in this hobby, and once you get the hang of things, you are going to find that it is easier than ever to get started with your own projects.

Remember that each of these knots is going to be the foundation of the other projects that you create, so you are going to have to take the time to get familiar with each of them – and practice them until they are what you need them to be. You are not likely going to get them perfectly right away – so take the time to make sure you do it right before you move on to the succeeding one.

Do not worry if you do not get it at first, it is going to come with time, and the more time you put into it, the better you are going to become. It does take time and effort to get it right, but the more time and effort you put into it, the better you are going to be. My goal with this is to give you the inspiration and direction you need to master macramé.

It can be difficult at first, but the more you put into it, the easier it is all going to become until it is just second nature to you. I know you are going to fall in love with each and every aspect of this hobby, and when you know how to work the knots, you are going to want to make them in all the ways you possibly can.

Do not worry about the colors, and do not worry if you do not get it right the first time. This is going to give you everything you need to make it happen the way you want it to, and it is going to show you that you really can have it all with your macramé projects.

I hope you become a master at this hobby, and that you can get the projects you want from the patterns you use. There is no end to the ways you can create macramé projects, and the more familiar you become with them; the easier it is going to be for you to make them no matter what you want them to be. So, dive into the world of macramé with both feet, and learn that there is nothing that is going to stand in your way when it comes to these projects.

So, what are you waiting for? All it is going to take is your time and effort, and you are going to get just what you are after with your macramé projects. From now on, you are on the path to be a macramé master, and you are going to fall in love with everything macramé. The world of macramé awaits, just begging you to dive in and get started.

Good luck and create to your heart's content.

So, stay sharp, keep practicing and keep getting better. Welcome to a world of infinite possibilities!

Stop reading, start doing!

CPSIA information can be obtained
at www.ICGtesting.com
Printed in the USA
LVHW021808141120
671495LV00003B/201

9 781801 136730